About the author

Peter McManners works as an author, consultant and Visiting Fellow of Henley Business School, Reading University. He is a member of the Institute for Green Economics and has published extensively on business and environment.

PETER MCMANNERS

Fly and be damned

what now for aviation and climate change?

Zed Books
LONDON | NEW YORK

Fly and be damned: what now for aviation and climate change? was first published in 2012 by Zed Books Ltd, 7 Cynthia Street, London N1 9JF, UK and Room 400, 175 Fifth Avenue, New York, NY 10010, USA

www.zedbooks.co.uk

Set in Monotype Sabon and Gill Sans Heavy by Ewan Smith, London
Index: ed.emery@thefreeuniversity.net
Cover designed by Kika Sroka-Miller www.kikamiller.com
Printed and bound in Great Britain by MPG Books Group, Bodmin and King's Lynn

Distributed in the USA exclusively by Palgrave Macmillan, a division of St Martin's Press, LLC, 175 Fifth Avenue, New York, NY 10010, USA

A catalogue record for this book is available from the British Library
Library of Congress Cataloging in Publication Data available

ISBN 978 1 84813 975 6 hb
ISBN 978 1 84813 974 9 pb

Contents

Abbreviations

BA	British Airways
CAA	Civil Aviation Authority
EU	European Union
EU ETS	EU Emissions Trading Scheme
FAA	Federal Aviation Administration
GDP	gross domestic product
GHG	greenhouse gas
HULA	Hybrid Ultra Large Aircraft
IATA	International Air Transport Association
ICAO	International Civil Aviation Organization
IMF	International Monetary Fund
IPCC	Intergovernmental Panel on Climate Change
NASA	National Aeronautics and Space Administration
OPEC	Organization of the Petroleum Exporting Countries
PRC	People's Republic of China
SDC	Sustainable Development Commission
SSEE	Smith School of Enterprise and the Environment
UN	United Nations
UNEP	United Nations Environment Programme
UNFCCC	United Nations Framework Convention on Climate Change
WTO	World Trade Organization

Preface

This book is about a revolution in aviation to set it on a new path which reconciles the benefits with the imperative to reduce its environmental impact. The changes required are an important aspect of the transition to a sustainable world society.

Adopting the paradigm of sustainability, in which quality of life and sound environmental policy go hand in hand, requires complex change that reaches across all industrial sectors and will affect every community. There are few single-issue solutions, as everything interconnects. The changes are doable, but require a sweeping transformation throughout society and the economy, which I describe as the Sustainable Revolution (McManners 2008). Policy-makers have avoided confronting the challenge of reducing the environmental impact of aviation, ensnaring aviation in an outdated policy framework, such that when the Sustainable Revolution plays out, the aviation industry, and our expectations of it, will have to change dramatically.

When respect for the ecosystem is taught in primary schools and the concepts of sustainability are ingrained in secondary schools, people will understand and accept the need for change. When university courses across the range, from economics and business to engineering and politics, include a core module on sustainability, the concepts used in this book will be second nature to the professionals who run society, but the current state of aviation policy is an example of the current lack of deep knowledge. It will take time before the education system provides the deep understanding that allows the concepts of sustainability to migrate into the DNA of society.

A sustainable future will be a better future, but not in every way. Putting a higher priority on social outcomes, within the context of safeguarding the environment, leads to improved quality of life but it also leads to reining back on material consumption. The knee-jerk reaction is to complain, but this has to be resisted to remain open minded to a better but different way to run society. This is particularly true for aviation.

Aviation is a special case of sustainable policy formulation for two reasons. First, making aviation much less reliant on fossil fuel requires a step-change in technology that involves developing and deploying a new fleet of air vehicles. Second, the rich world's expectations of flying are so deeply ingrained that, on the route to a sustainable society, aviation policy is the most difficult nut to crack. I also realized that getting at the kernel of this problem, and solving it, could be the trigger for wider change in society, showing that the difficult challenges of sustainability are not impossible.

Developments in aviation, which could deliver high-quality sustainable flying, are being held back by the protection afforded by the Chicago Convention, dating from 1944, which ensures that aviation fuel for international flights is tax free. This is environmentally indefensible but regarded widely as politically untouchable. This can change if world leaders, under the cover of collective responsibility, decide to act.

The conclusions I draw do not fit with current accepted policy, and will therefore be resisted. Even among environmentalists there are some who have been persuaded that aviation should be exempt from tough environmental controls, because flying would become less affordable for many people. It has become an intractable problem because it has been framed as a conflict between progress and environmental stewardship. This needs to be reframed as an alliance such that the next phase of aviation is a leap forward to a better aviation industry in which stewardship of the environment is integral.

This book is aimed at a wide audience because action will come about only through a whole series of individual choices to support change and accept the consequences. It is not my intention to offend anyone, any group or any organization, but I expose some inconvenient truths that have been swept under a carpet of vested interests and lazy politicking. Some people will choose to take offence at my words, worried at the consequences for them or the organization they represent. I hope that there are others who will be invigorated by my call to set free forces that will reconfigure aviation to be fit for the twenty-first century. The result will be a sustainable aviation industry and a better flying experience.

to Tiina

Introduction

Aviation is caught in a dilemma, with policy-makers torn between supporting continued expansion and the need to address the sector's environmental impact. Social and economic benefits accrue from flying but the associated emissions are causing damage to the atmosphere. The looming dangers of climate change mean that this dilemma must be resolved.

In Part 1, a snapshot of aviation shows that it is one of the fastest-growing sources of greenhouse gas emissions. These emissions, particularly carbon dioxide (CO_2) but also other pollutants, are damaging the atmosphere and causing changes to the climate. Concern is growing and evidence that the problems could be serious is starting to emerge, but society is not yet ready to take the action that will reconcile people's addiction to flying (Chapter 1) with sound environmental policy. As long as climate change, examined in Chapter 2, is seen as a problem that will affect another generation, some time in the future, politicians lack a compelling reason to risk unpopularity by changing policy and controlling the projected expansion of aviation (Chapter 3).

The emissions from aviation are at high altitude, out of sight, out of mind and out of control. There is a widespread attitude of fly and be damned.

In Part 2, the current status of world aviation is examined, starting with, in Chapter 4, an outline of the progress that was made through the twentieth century from the Wright brothers' first tentative flight to the launch of the space age. Throughout this period the key developments often came about out of crisis (Chapter 5); the next leap forward in aviation could well be in response to the climate crisis. Such an advance would require reform of the linchpin of aviation policy, the Convention on International Civil

Aviation, agreed in Chicago in December 1944. This convention, discussed in Chapter 6, still rules international aviation today and holds the industry in an outdated policy framework in which aviation fuel for international flights is free of tax. This not only boosts growth (as the delegates at Chicago in 1944 intended) but also acts as a barrier to the development of aviation that is less reliant on fossil fuel. With fuel so cheap, it is not cost effective to make substantial investments in greener aviation.

In Chapter 7, the relationship between globalization and aviation is discussed, followed by an examination of the growth of low-cost aviation (Chapter 8) and the associated hazards. It is becoming clear that the current mould of aviation must be broken, explained in Chapter 9, but the situation is not seen as a crisis and policy-makers are slow to appreciate the degree of change required. In Chapter 10, measures are considered, ranging from improved aircraft efficiency and better air traffic control to operational efficiencies and the introduction of biofuel. This examination shows that the measures currently under discussion are too little, too late.

Part 3 looks to the future, when it becomes economically viable to replace conventional aircraft with a fleet of green air vehicles (Chapter 11), launching the third golden age of aviation (Chapter 12). This can come about through unleashing the entrepreneurs who can make the vision of sustainable aviation a reality (Chapter 13). One aspect of the transformation will be the resurgence of trains as a viable alternative to short-haul flights (Chapter 14), although the long time frame and high levels of investment will be a challenge.

Once it becomes clear to the majority of people that the impact of climate change will be significant, with damaging consequences for society, politicians will be forced to move quickly beyond the painstaking climate debate taking place under the auspices of the United Nations. The circumstances will arise for bold action, including calling for a new convention on civil aviation that can deliver a policy framework fit for the twenty-first century (Chapter 15).

The key tool of policy to force the transformation will be agreement to introduce taxation on aviation fuel, with the dual aims of constraining capacity in the short term and supporting the development of commercially viable sustainable aviation for the future. This measure will underpin the development of green air vehicles as part of the next golden age of aviation as the changed economic parameters unleash a surge of innovation. The transition to twenty-first-century aviation will not be smooth, and may not be easy, requiring a break with the policy of the past. As world leaders continue to fail to agree effective controls on CO_2 emissions, and direct evidence of climate change grows stronger, the debate will turn from talk about long-term targets to near-term urgent action. That will be when the future of twenty-first-century aviation will be decided.

ONE | **Fly and be damned**

1 | Addicted to flying

Thank God men cannot as yet fly and lay waste the sky
as well as the earth.   Henry Thoreau (1861)

Aviation is a showcase of civilization, demonstrating human ability to harness advanced technology to improve people's lives. The complex global web of aviation services shows how, working together on a common objective, human society can achieve incredible advances. That single-minded focus, which brings such success, can also make us blind to the wider consequences. The time has come to open our eyes to the impact of the emissions from flying and collaborate to make aviation fit for the twenty-first century.

Charles Lindbergh, an early pioneer of aviation, was one of the first people to question its environmental impact. Famous for being the first to fly solo non-stop from New York to Paris, he went on to promote the development of US commercial aviation in the 1920s before later in life becoming an environmentalist. In his book *Of Flight and Life* (1948) he wrote about the two great passions of his life: flying and the environment. From retirement on the Hawaiian island of Maui, he reflected on the priority between them: 'If I had to choose, I would rather have birds than airplanes' (Lindbergh 1964).

Charles Lindbergh died in 1974, so he did not witness the huge expansion of aviation over the last few decades. I believe he would have been impressed, but also hugely disappointed that so little had been done to reduce the environmental impact.

In this chapter it is shown that aviation has become so large and so pervasive that it is time to reflect on priorities. The problem is not flying, as much as the impact of current fossil-fuel propulsion technology. For us to continue to fly with a clear conscience, aviation must become less reliant on fossil fuel. This is not a simple modification; not only are new aircraft required, but people's expectations must change.

The aviation debate

The policy options for aviation and the environment are highly contested (Walker and Cook 2009). The debate has polarized into a pro-flying lobby that seek to exempt aviation from paying for its environmental impact and an anti-flying lobby that avoid flying and expect others to follow their example. The UK's Sustainable Development Commission (SDC) carried out an extensive stakeholder assessment of aviation and recorded highly divergent views (SDC 2008). From these entrenched positions it is hard to see how to make progress. There are very few people in the middle arguing for flying but demanding that it be green. The debate has to move forward from defence of, or opposition to, the status quo to focus on the nature and shape of aviation within a sustainable society.

Aviation is here to stay, but the aviation industry and the options available to passengers cannot remain the same if the dilemma between the desire to fly and environmental responsibility is to be resolved. The changes required to migrate away from fossil fuel are not easy and it is necessary to look past the short term to appreciate the changes as progress. If the pro-flying lobby would accept the need for change and the anti-flying lobby engage with shaping policy then aviation could be made better and greener.

There is a sustainable aviation business waiting to take off but it is grounded by the heavy baggage of a range of vested interests. Airlines are preoccupied with tight margins and cut-throat competition. Aircraft manufacturers are struggling to secure sales of current models and wary of making risky new investments. Governments are scared of the possible economic consequences and fear an electoral backlash if they force change. Progress is stalled until measures like those outlined in this book are accepted and implemented.

People like to fly and welcome the general trend over recent decades that flying has been getting cheaper. As a business person, if there is a problem in the supply chain it is possible to hop on a long-haul flight to Hong Kong to meet a representative of the Chinese supplier.[1] If necessary, it is easy to transfer to a regional flight to visit the factory in mainland China in person. As a tourist from a developed economy, exploring other countries and other continents is easy; the main constraint is not the price but being able to book enough days of holiday. Flights are affordable and reliable with all the major cities of the world reachable within twenty-four hours' flying time.

The reason for flying may be a simple desire for reliable weather. People from New York would rather travel to Florida than to Martha's Vineyard. Residents of London would rather travel to the Costa del Sol than to Brighton. Sea and sandy beaches are to be found closer to home, but it costs little more to travel farther south by low-cost carrier, where the sun is more reliable.

Price is a consideration when choosing the destination and airline, but price is no longer a strong factor influencing behaviour. Very few people question whether to fly. For people on a tight budget, it is necessary to book well in advance with low-cost airlines flying out of regional airports. Often, such flights are not only the cheapest flights but the cheapest of all travel options as low-cost airlines strive to undercut the ticket prices for ground transportation.

The environmental impact of flying is growing in people's awareness but is not high on most people's personal priorities. Airlines have brought in voluntary carbon offset schemes to allow passengers to choose to pay a small premium to offset the carbon emitted in making their flight. The take-up has been 'disappointing', as BA's company secretary, Alan Buchanan, put it to a House of Commons select committee in 2007. He explained that BA had brought in a voluntary offset scheme in 2005 but passengers had

1 The example of outsourcing production to China is used to resonate with current business issues. Of course, the model of remote outsourcing will change as the sustainability agenda starts to drive policy; shorter supply chains will be one consequence.

chosen to purchase only 1,600 tonnes of offsets on average each year, approximately the emissions from four return flights to New York (House of Commons 2007).

When flying is examined through the lens of self-interest there is little incentive to change. It is difficult to argue that passengers should choose to pay for an offset when the passenger beside them has not.

Some changes in aviation are relatively easy, such as marginally more efficient conventional aircraft and improved air traffic control. These are changes that should be made, but in an industry expected to expand, the total effects will be little more than swimming against the tide.

Aviation and sustainability

Achieving a sustainable future for civilization is the prime challenge of the twenty-first century, which means, in simple terms, implementing policy that balances social, environmental and economic factors. Sustainability also includes the concept of society continuing into the future, which has been described as meeting the 'needs of the present without compromising the ability of future generations to meet their own needs' (WCED 1987).

Policy-makers are slowly coming to terms with the implications of adopting sustainability. There are few easy solutions to initiating change on the scale required within the massively complex systems of modern society. Mr Ahmed Djoghlaf, the executive secretary of the Convention on Biological Diversity, summed up the challenge in a speech at the 2nd International Conference on Sustainable Business and Consumption, held in Nuremberg, Germany, in June 2010 (Djoghlaf 2010):

> today more than ever we need another Renaissance – a modern rebirth of human society. Today more than ever, when we are systematically destroying life on this planet through our own short-sightedness ... we need to comprehensively rethink our place in, and our interactions with, Nature.

One symptom of the pressure being placed on the global ecosystem is climate change. An understanding of the dangers has migrated from the science community into the public domain through messengers like Al Gore (2006). This is progress, but it is proving hard to translate concern into effective policy.

The role of aviation in climate change is important but has been downplayed. There has been a tendency to regard the emissions from flying as a small proportion of the global total and therefore not significant. My analysis disputes this and concurs with recent research that making aviation a special case is not justified (Gössling and Upham 2009).

If world society is serious about sustainability, aviation has to be tackled. This sector is capital intensive with long lead times, so the policy framework has to be in place early to start a transformation that will take decades to complete. There is also the expectation of enormous growth in emerging markets; if this expansion takes place within the existing policy framework, countries will be lumbered with expensive outdated infrastructure. Failure to tackle aviation will also be a very strong indication of likely failure to make real progress with other areas of sustainable policy. Grasping this nettle is the test of our resolve. It will not be easy, but success will set the circumstances in which action to address a whole raft of other aspects of sustainable society will become possible.

Effective action with regard to aviation could be the trigger that initiates the Sustainable Revolution. It would show that the world can take politically difficult decisions, demonstrating leadership and commitment. This trigger effect has the potential to deliver greater carbon reductions than the reductions attributable directly to greener aviation.

Resistance to change

The SDC stakeholder assessment (SDC 2008) found that the area where there was most controversy was around the 'right' and 'need' to fly. It is human nature to defend what we have and to resist attempts to take away what people regard as their rights. This applies to a whole range of activities from terms of employment to the freedom to drive cars where and when we wish. This attitude also extends to affordable flying, which is now ingrained in society as a right to be defended. When it is suggested that a job description is out of date and that it must be rewritten, the employee worries about the possible outcome and therefore resists. When it is suggested that access for cars should be restricted, the first reaction is to oppose, unless it can be shown that benefits flow back into the local community through safer and more pleasant streets. To suggest that flying should be greener to protect the global ecosystem is a hard concept to sell without generating resistance.

It will not be easy to persuade individuals to support policy that will make flying more expensive. Governments are wary of forcing the issue when the advantages accrue only at the global level. The benefits are too far into the future and too removed from people's everyday lives to overcome the instinctive reaction to resist.

Conventional flying has developed a reliance on cheap aviation fuel and a range of subsidies. If the full environmental costs are brought into the calculation, flying will be more expensive. A common response to this insight is to object on the grounds that to implement the required taxes or charges would mean that only the rich could afford to fly. Other political options are considered, such as rationing flying in some way, perhaps through a system of personal carbon allowances. Such ideas are interesting but tend to act as a distraction.

Looking more closely at the cohort of people who fly, these are the relatively rich people of the world. No one in real need, or struggling to survive, is an airline passenger. Arguments are put forward that there are poor people (less rich) for whom the cost of flying should be kept low. There are isolated examples where this is true, but in my experience such arguments do not stand up to rigorous analysis.

There is no justification for sheltering aviation from the full cost of its environmental impact. However, the notion of unfairness is very strong. People would be justified in complaining if increasing costs to the correct level was confined to one group.

It is important to ensure that appropriate measures apply across society and across international boundaries so that everyone who flies shoulders the burden of increased costs. This is one of the challenges, but the solution is possible if there is political will.

Beyond the conventional view

A recent in-depth analysis of low-carbon flying took place at the World Forum on Enterprise and the Environment 2010, hosted by the Smith School of Enterprise and the Environment (SSEE), Oxford University. This event is becoming as important among the green business community as the World Economic Forum at Davos is among economists. The theme was 'Low Carbon Mobility: Land, Sea and Air'.

Among the group of experts in the Air Working Group, the conventional economic context was accepted as a fixed constraint, with the consequence that many potential solutions were ruled out. At the end of the conference the rapporteur summed up the findings, concluding that the emphasis should be on consultation with passengers to test what they want and will accept. This was a business-as-usual perspective, illustrating how business designs products and tweaks the specification to suit customer preferences. This is about as far as business can go, working alone, to make progress towards low-carbon aviation.

It is necessary to step back from an industry perspective and consider aviation from the perspective of society. Securing the future of society requires that policy-makers learn and implement the policies of sustainability. Such policy requires the greening of aviation. If world governments can find a way to move in concert to shape the future of sustainable aviation, industry and customers will have to fall into line.

It is possible for the governments of the world to move together on this issue but the required measures may be unpopular in the short term. This can lead to avoidance of the difficult and necessary policy decisions because of expected opposition. Aviation is not unique; there are a number of areas of the transition to a sustainable society that will need bolder leadership than is

13

common in modern democratic politics, dominated by feedback from focus groups. Ways must be found to force through policy despite expected negative reactions. Action may be delayed until a shared desire to respond to environmental challenges grows within society, reaching a tipping point which gives governments the mandate to implement potentially unpopular measures.

Real action

Removing the constraint of artificially low fuel prices will provide the circumstances to transform the industry. Many companies that fail to read the future will fold, causing disruption, but the positive outcome will be that aeronautical engineers will be set free to design and develop the prototypes that are needed for green air vehicles. We can look forward to a renaissance in aviation as green innovation takes off.

The rich countries have an opportunity to lead, with the prospect of leveraging much wider change in society than the particular changes made in aviation. Effective action with regard to aviation will demonstrate resolve and commitment to tackle other areas of the economy. Poorer countries are more likely to fall in line behind the efforts of the developed world to constrain CO_2 emissions when they observe action to address the global impact of aviation – a sector dominated by the richer countries.

Each stakeholder in aviation will have reasons not to like the analysis in this book: aircraft manufacturers will be concerned that their product line-up will soon be out of date; airline bosses with short-term profit targets will worry that the revolution will hit before they have banked their bonuses; government ministers will be concerned at the impact on the economy and jobs; and passengers will complain at higher costs that do not connect with direct benefits to themselves. No one wants the rug pulled from under them, but the case for change is presented with confidence that the industry can reinvent itself to match altered circumstances. The outcome of taking bold action to address the environmental impact of aviation can be a greener and better aviation sector.

2 | Climate change

Action on climate is justified, not because the science is certain, but precisely because it is not.   Economist (2010a)

Emissions from aviation are one of the causes of climate change and the main concern is the rapid increase of recent years, which is forecast to continue. For example, carbon dioxide emissions from international aviation (excluding domestic aviation) were 455 Mt in 2008 (IEA 2010), an increase of 76 per cent compared with 1990. Total CO_2 emissions from aviation accounts for between 2 and 3 per cent of global CO_2 emissions, but if aviation is allowed to grow unchecked, these could increase substantially. Passenger traffic is expected to grow 5 per cent annually over the next twenty or twenty-five years, with freight growing slightly faster at 6 per cent annually. Figures reported by the IPCC 'suggest that total global aviation emissions were approximately 492 Mt CO_2 and 2.06 Mt NOx in 2002 and will increase to 1029 and 3.31 Mt respectively by 2025' (Kahn Ribeiro and Kobayashi 2007). A recent report from the OECD (2010) confirms that emissions from aviation in 2030 are expected to at least double from a 2002 baseline and could increase by a factor of 3.2. The report states that '... as long as the full external cost is not covered by the ticket price, environmental damage caused by aviation will continue to grow'. Figures from the UK are representative of the trend in developed economies, showing that total CO_2 emissions from domestic and international aviation attributable to the UK increased from around 7.29 Mt (1.0 per cent of the national total) in 1970, to 16.95 Mt (2.8 per cent of the total) in 1990, and further to 37.47 Mt (6.3 per cent of the total) in 2005 (Fullerton et al. 2010).

In this chapter, the science of climate change is reviewed, showing that the dangers are significant and that measures to counter the threat remain elusive. When world society wakes up to the dangers, real action will follow and the circumstances will arise to transform aviation to reduce its role in climate change.

Climate change and politics

Sir David King, Chief Scientific Adviser to the UK government 2000–08, made headlines around the world when he wrote in *Science* that 'climate change is the most severe problem that we are facing today – more serious even than the threat of terrorism' (King 2004). Former US vice-president Al Gore took the message to a wider audience with his lectures, book and film *An Inconvenient Truth* (Gore 2006). It certainly was an inconvenient message. If it was right, the world economy would have to embark on massive change. This truth is still being resisted today, but change is coming. Evidence of climate change is shifting from the computer models and scientific papers to observable changes in the real world.

The world has warmed by 0.76 degrees Celsius since the start of the Industrial Revolution.[1] From year to year there are variations but the trend is clear. The first decade of the twenty-first century was the warmest decade on record; before that it was the 1990s; before that the 1980s (Pope et al. 2008; Met Office 2009). The Intergovernmental Panel on Climate Change (IPCC) predictions include a range of scenarios indicating that temperatures will increase this century within the range 1.1–6.4 degrees, causing sea levels to rise in the range 0.18–0.59m (Meehl and Stocker 2007). The lower end of these predictions would not cause severe impacts but the upper end should be causing grave concern.

Underlying the huge amounts of research published in copious documents is the question 'Is this a risk we should be running?' Based on my knowledge of the science, my answer is 'No,' we should not be putting the climate at risk. Therefore, my personal view is that there is no need to wait until the evidence is exam-

---

1 'The total temperature increase from 1850–1899 to 2001–2005 is 0.76°C' (Solomon et al. 2007).

ined in yet greater detail; the deduction is clear: the fossil fuel economy must be dismantled without delay. However, I accept that there are many people who are not yet persuaded and could answer that maybe it is a risk worth running to retain our current lifestyles. This viewpoint requires that the risks are assessed carefully, based on the best available science, in the context of the long-term future for society and the environment.

The discussion about climate change focuses on greenhouse gases, in particular carbon dioxide. Over the last ten years the level of CO_2 in the atmosphere has increased on average 2 ppm annually. Each year, a new record level of CO_2 is set, reaching 388 ppm in 2009 (Tans 2010), higher than at any time over the last 800,000 years (Lüthi et al. 2008). In 2009, CO_2 emissions in China, the world's leading emitter, grew by nearly 9 per cent. At the same time, emissions in most industrial countries dropped, due to the recession, holding global CO_2 emissions from fossil fuel use level between 2008 and 2009. This pause in growth follows a decade of rapid growth; over the ten previous years, global CO_2 emissions rose by an average of 2.5 per cent a year, nearly four times as fast as in the 1990s (EIA 2011).

The 'safe' level of CO_2 in the atmosphere to prevent dangerous climate change is judged to be no more than 450–500 ppm. The experts predict that at this level global warming would be two degrees. Negotiations focus on the total cumulative CO_2 emissions that can be allowed to prevent exceeding this safe limit.

Business as usual will take CO_2 levels beyond the safe limit into a new climate that will be very different to today's. The outcome will be hard to determine. The situation is like dropping a massive bomb through heavy cloud on to a city. There is no way of knowing which buildings will be demolished and which left standing, but we can be almost certain the outcome will be bad. Continuing down the route of business as usual to global temperature rises of three, four, five degrees or beyond will have irreversible consequences for the Earth. Speculating on the detail of just how bad it could be is useful in raising the public consciousness (Lynas 2007) and reminding policy-makers that

17

the 'safe limit' of two degrees must be used as the cornerstone of policy.

The Kyoto Protocol, linked to the UN Framework Convention on Climate Change (UNFCCC), will soon have run its course. It is an international agreement to reduce greenhouse gas (GHG) emissions by an average of 5 per cent against 1990 levels over the five-year period 2008–12. Discussions over a successor agreement have been difficult and slow.

The limited progress at the talks in Cancún in December 2010 does not bode well. The parties agreed that 'deep cuts in global greenhouse gas emissions are required ... to hold the increase in global average temperature below 2°C above pre-industrial levels'. They also agreed 'to work towards identifying a global goal for substantially reducing global emissions by 2050' (UNFCCC 2010). Such limited progress after more than a decade of discussion would suggest that the result of the UNFCCC negotiations is likely to be a set of weak targets, which are not enforceable, and which the world will overshoot as the target dates approach. Yvo de Boer summed up the situation well when he stepped down as head of the UN climate change secretariat in the summer of 2010: 'I don't see the process delivering adequate mitigation targets in the next decade' (Murray 2010).

The debate hides the uncertainty that accompanies the headline figures for total global emissions. Assuming that the world focuses on the 'safe limit' of two degrees, and the world implements a limit of 1,440 Gt CO_2 of cumulative emissions over the period 2000–50, there is a 50 per cent probability of warming exceeding two degrees. If the limit is set lower at 1,000 Gt CO_2 there is still a 25 per cent probability that two degrees will be exceeded (Meinshausen et al. 2009). Uncertainty can be used by sceptics to delay action, but uncertainty also means that emission targets set now might not be tough enough.

Time frame is also important, with long time frames needed in assessing the consequences of climate change out to a century or more. On the other hand, short time frames are needed in considering policy options to hold governments to account.

The political decision to focus targets on 2050 is a compromise. This is too short a time frame to capture the true gravity of the challenge and too long to hold governments to account for their promises. Scenarios reaching out to 2050 can be constructed that allow continued growth in emissions in the near term provided that massive reductions are made later in the period. This is politically convenient but also hides the urgency of acting sooner. The date 2020 should be used more widely to bring clarity and realism to the debate. Meinshausen et al. (ibid.) assess that the probability of exceeding two degrees this century rises to over 50 per cent if global GHG emissions are still more than 25 per cent above 2000 levels in 2020, a limit already breached in 2009 (EIA 2011). To peg global carbon emissions and prevent further increase would require urgent action now.

The world-level negotiations are held back because climate change is not seen as a crisis. Despite the warnings, world leaders are slow to accept responsibility for changing course; the problems are in the future, action is therefore delayed into the future. It will be no consolation to look back from the future wishing that action had been initiated sooner. The response has to be now if dangerous climate change is to be prevented. This simple message should be communicated loud and clear, but climate sceptics have had success in injecting doubt into the public consciousness.

Climate tipping points

It is necessary to reach way back into geological time for circumstances that are similar to those today. The fossil record shows that about fifty-five million years ago an event called the Paleocene-Eocene Thermal Maximum (PETM) occurred. At that time, temperatures rose rapidly by as much as 10 degrees at high latitudes in the Arctic and Antarctic. Tropical oceans and deep-ocean waters warmed by between four and six degrees. This was accompanied by dramatic effects on plants and animals. Scientists think that the fast-changing climate was driven by a natural release of carbon-containing greenhouse gases comparable

19

to what has been occurring with the release of CO_2 and other gases since the start of the Industrial Revolution.

We should be very worried. The relatively low levels of global warming being observed in these early stages of climate change may be enough to start the process of thawing frozen deposits of methane hydrates. These are present in vast quantities as frozen sediments in the deep oceans, and some are associated with permafrost soils in the Arctic. Warming of the oceans and the Arctic region could release sufficient methane to initiate a positive feedback effect, releasing still more gas as ocean waters and permafrost regions continue to warm. Methane is a much more potent greenhouse gas than CO_2. The theory is that the process reaches a tipping point when it starts to accelerate rapidly, without any way to stop the process, until the world reaches a new, and much hotter, equilibrium.

The Paleocene-Eocene Thermal Maximum is proof that the Earth's system does have tipping points, which, when exceeded, can quickly lead to a new and different equilibrium. Exactly why these past episodes have occurred is subject to much speculation. Scientists can use bubbles of air trapped in the deep Antarctic ice to investigate ancient climate history, but this takes them back only 800,000 years. This is not far enough. Scientists cannot prove that the world's climate is, or is not, reaching a tipping point. The point that should concern us most is that if we are pushing against a tipping point, and we find it, there will be nothing we can do to stop the runaway climate change that would follow. Runaway climate change would be disastrous; we should not be taking such a risk, but the risk is unquantifiable.

Abrupt climate change

Scientists are concerned about a number of abrupt changes that could be brought about by the warming climate, including the possibility that the Gulf Stream, which keeps Europe warm, might shut down (unlikely) or of more extreme weather events due to changes to the El Niño/La Niña-Southern Oscillation – a climate pattern that occurs across the tropical Pacific Ocean.

There are also concerns that the Amazon rainforest could shrink dramatically if global temperatures were to rise beyond four degrees. Rising sea level is another concern, particularly if either the Greenland or West Antarctic ice sheets were to disappear. Each possible mechanism is subject to complex argument that requires considerable expertise to form a balanced judgement.

Abrupt climate change is possible, and if it were to occur the consequences would be severe. It is therefore important to examine the best available evidence. The scientists of Working Group I to the Fourth Assessment Report of the IPCC conclude that abrupt climate change is not likely to occur in the twenty-first century:

> Abrupt climate changes, such as the collapse of the West Antarctic Ice Sheet, the rapid loss of the Greenland Ice Sheet or large-scale changes of ocean circulation systems, are not considered likely to occur in the 21st century, based on currently available model results. However, the occurrence of such changes becomes increasingly more likely as the perturbation of the climate system progresses. (Meehl and Stocker 2007: 818–19)

Scientists of the IPCC take the examination of the evidence farther to conclude that the threshold could be crossed this century, beyond which the Greenland Ice Sheet would be committed to disappearing completely. The total melting of the Greenland Ice Sheet would be a slow process that would take many hundreds of years to complete. There is evidence that southern Greenland was covered by forest within the last million years (Willerslev et al. 2007). In a warming climate, the ice sheet might retreat and the forests return.

The melting of the entire Greenland Ice Sheet would raise global sea levels by about seven metres. This should make us pause to think, as seven metres has massive implications. This would require the relocation of many international cities, including much of London and New York. Hundreds of years seems like a long time to each one of us, but in the life of the world's cities it is a short window.

Greenland is not the only ice sheet to worry about. The warming climate may destabilize the West Antarctic Ice Sheet. If it were to collapse, that is another five to six metres of potential sea-level rise.

> Recent satellite and in situ observations of ice streams behind disintegrating ice shelves highlight some rapid reactions of ice sheet systems. This raises new concern about the overall stability of the West Antarctic Ice Sheet, the collapse of which would trigger another five to six metres of sea level rise. (Meehl and Stocker 2007)

Probability of abrupt climate change

There is a credible risk that the climate may be approaching a tipping when one or more abrupt changes occur. There is no way of determining a firm probability for such an event as, during the period for which we have measurements, the climate has not passed a tipping point; so there are no comparative data.

Risk analysis is a mature discipline used widely in commercial decision-making. Unusual events, for which there are no historical data, require a special approach. Recent research by Kriegler et al. (2009) carried out such an analysis. They have taken the expert opinions of the world's leading climate scientists (forty-three in total) about their assessment of the likelihood of abrupt climate change. They have taken account of a range of certainty and then used statistical methods on the data to come up with a balanced judgement. Each individual view does not constitute proof, but when they are taken together the result is compelling.

The conclusions of the research indicate that there is a significant risk of abrupt climate change. The researchers deduce that if emissions are controlled sufficiently to hold global warming in the range two to four degrees (relative to year 2000), the probability of triggering at least one abrupt climate change event is approximately one in six (0.16). If emissions continue at a level that leads to a global mean temperature rise above four degrees, the probability is greater than one in two (0.56).

The Arctic as an indicator

The changes that will happen in the Arctic over the coming decades will show graphically that the planet will indeed change as a consequence of climate change. There are feedback effects in the Arctic that are well understood which are speeding up climate change. White ice reflects energy from the sun back into space. As the polar ice retreats each summer, it is replaced with open water. This dark water absorbs the sun's energy, enhancing the local effect of global warming. The Arctic region is not highly populous and the effects may not impact the majority of human society. Research is looking beyond whether the Arctic will change, to how people and society will have to adjust (UNESCO 2009). One probable effect will be that the polar bear will become extinct in the wild. To environmentalists, the fate of the polar bear will become a symbol that civilization has set the wrong priorities. Others are already welcoming the opportunity to exploit an ice-free Arctic Ocean to be able to extract the oil and gas beneath and open the Northwest Passage (a sea route around the top of Canada).

It is a sobering thought that even rapid change in the Arctic may not be enough to stir the world into action.

To act or not to act, that is the question

The science leaves room for entrenched views at each end of the spectrum. The doom mongers claim that the planet is on the verge of an irreversible massive shift in the climate, with potentially severe consequences. The climate sceptics point out that there is uncertainty in the science.

Whether you believe the predictions of massive climate change or are sceptical, the outcome should be much the same. Driving in fog is a useful analogy to draw out the logic. Sensible drivers do not drive at high speed into thick fog. It is likely that the road is clear but the chance that there may be a stationary vehicle is a risk that is not worth taking. Some drivers gamble that there is only a one-in-a-hundred, or one-in-a-thousand, chance that the road is not clear and so press on. This is not a sensible gamble

23

but it can be understood. Each time the risk is taken the chances are that the driver will survive. Brash young men in fast cars take the risk and some die, but most learn a more cautious approach as they survive and get older. Gambling with climate change – which is what climate sceptics are doing – has very different odds. The judgement of scientists is that there is a 50 per cent chance that global warming will exceed the 'safe' limit of two degrees if carbon emissions are not capped within the next decade. To the cocky driver with a new sports car, odds of 50 per cent that there is a stationary truck ahead will force even the most daring driver to slow down. It is not a risk worth taking.

Another analogy brings yet more clarity to the nature of our actions (inactions) over climate change. Russian roulette is a game only for the foolhardy. A revolver is loaded with one bullet. Each player spins the cylinder before holding the gun to their head and pulling the trigger. Typically a cylinder has holes for six cartridges. There is therefore a chance of one in six on each turn that the player will die. This is about the same odds that Kriegler et al. (2009) assessed of abrupt climate change for global warming in the range two to four degrees. Extreme risk takers may take pleasure in such a game provided it is a rare example of bravado that does not have to be repeated. The chances are the player will survive.

The sceptics who argue against action to reduce fossil fuel dependency, and therefore gamble with the risk that global warming could exceed four degrees, are playing with worse odds than a driver going fast in heavy fog while simultaneously having a gun to the head in a game of Russian roulette. The driver is more likely to survive such a prank than humankind has of avoiding the severe consequences of climate change if the sceptics win the argument.

I have used these analogies to try to draw the debate away from future-gazing into a recognizable real-world context based on odds derived from rigorous risk analysis, presented in a way that can be immediately understood. These analogies show that to demand incontrovertible proof of severe consequences of climate change, before taking action, makes no sense; but people need tangible evidence, not logical argument.

World society wakes up

While climate talks are a discussion about a projected future crisis, huff and puff is tolerated. When there are real effects impacting on people's lives, the world will move beyond the rhetoric to action. In 2003, a heat wave gripped Europe, claiming over thirty thousand lives and costing the economy 13 billion euros (de Bono et al. 2004). Two years later Hurricane Katrina hit the coast of Louisiana, devastating New Orleans and claiming over 1,800 lives (Knabb et al. 2005). These events cannot be attributed directly to climate change, but it is known that since the 1970s the number of such extreme weather events has been rising (IPCC 2007). At the very least, these incidents are a reminder of the power of nature, and that nowhere will be immune from the consequences of climate change.

Extreme weather is still regarded as an act of God in the public psyche. On 19 November 2009, Cumbria in the UK had 316 mm of rain (Met Office 2010). This is the heaviest rainfall recorded in the UK since meteorologists started using instruments to record rainfall back in 1727. Twenty bridges were destroyed, 661 homes flooded and the total cost was £276 million (Wainwright 2010). This was not a disaster when viewed from a global perspective, but if incidents like these become commonplace, and it becomes accepted that human-induced climate change is making them more likely, attitudes will change. People will expect politicians to act.

Real action

The world is approaching peak oil production, when supply will not be able to expand to satisfy increasing demand. When that happens, the $147 dollar a barrel record set in 2008 will soon be surpassed as countries and corporations bid for the supplies they need. The relatively benign energy market will not continue. Action over climate change needs to happen now while oil is still easily affordable to make the transition without severe hardship.

The cost of building a low-carbon economy may seem high, but there is room in the economy to raise taxes and divert investment to make the transition away from fossil fuel. This window of opportunity will not be open for long. When oil prices surge higher, it will be politically hard to push prices even higher through taxation.

It will require massive change to reduce quickly society's reliance on fossil fuel. It is therefore understandable that world leaders are reluctant to act; but it is no longer credible to deny that the world faces crisis. The need to act is evident. There is a strong argument that action should be independent of the detailed analysis of climate change because the risks are too high to tolerate. Early action is desirable because we still have reserves of the cleaner fuels, such as gas, to cushion the transition.

The debate over climate change will produce ever more detailed analysis and scenario planning. This should continue, to find out more, compare real data with the predictions as each year goes by, and refine the models of the future climate. But there is no need to wait; we already know enough.

Failure to control CO_2 emissions from fossil fuel over the coming decades will cause dangerous climate change. Weak controls that slow CO_2 emissions, but do not reverse society's reliance on fossil fuel still run a risk of abrupt climate change events that would have catastrophic consequences for some regions. These are not risks that society should be taking with the future.

It is astounding that policy-makers remain deaf to calls for substantive action to deal with a ruinous crisis being played out in slow time in front of the world when the solutions, although not easy, are there to be grasped. We are all complicit in allowing the debate about climate change to produce more hot air than action.

3 | Projected expansion of capacity

Airports report worldwide passenger numbers in excess of 4.8 billion and total air cargo volumes of 86 million tonnes (ACI 2009). Predictions based on arithmetic projections of business-as-usual are indicating massive expansion of aviation over the next few decades. One prediction comes from the director general of the International Air Transport Association (IATA) in launching the 'IATA Vision 2050' in Berlin in June 2010 (Bisignani 2010). He forecast that by 2050 passenger numbers will climb to 16 billion and air cargo increase to 400 million tonnes. The IATA bases this on the assumption that the world middle class will nearly triple from 1.3 to 3.5 billion people with India and China accounting for a quarter of these potential travellers.

As populous developing countries become more affluent, a higher proportion of the population can afford to fly. When people's core needs for food and accommodation are secure they are able to contemplate discretionary expenditure, such as flying abroad as a tourist to explore the world. This expansion in people's aspirations is catching up with lifestyles that richer nations take for granted, bringing stark clarity to the problem of an aviation industry dependent on fossil fuel. The problem is not increased affluence in poorer countries, which should be welcomed for the benefits it brings to human welfare, but the outdated model for aviation which links growth directly with negative environmental impact. From a passenger perspective flying continues to improve: check-in gets slicker and more automated, more routes are opening and capacity expands. Demand grows as flying becomes more affordable to more people. Unless some sort of brake is applied the boom in flying seen over the last four decades is just the beginning of a huge further expansion.

In this chapter, it is shown that flying has become a routine and reliable backbone to the globalized world economy. As world GDP grows, aviation is expected to expand, particularly in the high-growth countries of the developing world. Aviation is locked into an economic model of rapid expansion and substantial growth of emissions.

Projecting future expansion becomes self-fulfilling. The projections are used by policy-makers in deciding the number and capacity of airports and by airlines in fleet purchase decisions. For projections to have true value, they should include deeper insight into issues such as the economic changes that adopting the paradigm of sustainability will entail, including the imperative to reduce the environmental impact of aviation.

Growth of CO_2 emissions

Flying accounts for around 2 per cent of global carbon dioxide emissions. This can be seen as 2 per cent too much, or a small percentage that can be ignored. Defenders of the current model of aviation argue that emissions from aviation should not be of great concern. They claim that it would be more effective to focus emission reductions on other sectors such as buildings and ground transportation where near-term reductions are easier to achieve, leaving aviation as a special case for exemption. This viewpoint has attraction, allowing policy-makers to steer clear of difficult decisions, but a close examination illustrates the danger of this abrogation of responsibility.

Aviation is an industry with long lead times, so failure to act now has long-term consequences. The figure to focus on is not current emissions but the future emissions that result from continuing with a business-as-usual policy template.

Emissions from aviation are expected to rise substantially, even after factoring in anticipated efficiency improvements in aircraft design and airline operations. According to a report for the UK Department of Transport, CO_2 emissions from international aviation may almost quadruple by 2050 to 1,442 Mt CO_2 compared with a 2006 baseline of 378 Mt CO_2 (Brannigan et al. 2009). This is the report's low estimate; its upper estimate is twice as much again, over 3,000 Mt CO_2 by 2050, a massive increase of eight times over 2006 emissions.

The developing world catches up

The developing world observes the richer countries and seeks to mimic their success. Aviation is not the sustainable choice to improve internal connections within large countries, but it is the obvious choice. Airports can be built quickly and cheaply in comparison with rail. Government investment can be low, relying on the private sector to establish the airlines. The private sector will expect tax-free aviation fuel (in line with international policy) and low airport charges. This model is being rolled out across China, India and other developing countries.

Liu Shaocheng, director of policy research at the Civil Aviation Administration of China, speaking at a conference in Beijing in July 2010, reported 266 million airline passengers in 2010 and forecast that number to more than double to 700 million by 2020; and it may double again to reach 1.5 billion by 2030. Liu Shaocheng expected that China would open up to ten new airports each year to have 250 airports by 2020 (compared with 176 at the end of 2010) (Bloomberg 2010).

Giovanni Bisignani, director general of the IATA, speaking at the Confederation of Indian Industry in New Delhi in September 2010, noted the tremendous potential for Indian aviation to grow from the current market of 42 million domestic and 34 million international passengers per year (IATA 2010a): 'If Indians flew as much as Americans, it would be a market of over 4 billion passengers. With the spending power of Indians set to triple over the next two years, the potential for growth is incredible.'

How the developing world approaches this potential for growth will be important to the overall environmental impact of world aviation over the next decade. Developing countries are likely to have limited existing transport infrastructure. Choices therefore remain open. These countries do not have the same path dependencies of developed countries held hostage to choices made back in history. India does not have to repeat the choices made by the United States or Europe.

Policy in support of domestic aviation also has the disadvantage for less developed countries that aircraft have to be purchased with foreign currency. Although in China, as it moves from a 'developing' to a 'developed' economy, its own aircraft industry is developing rapidly, and has been named a 'strategic emerging industry' by Liu Lihua, director of the general office of the PRC Ministry of Industry and Information Technology in a speech in November 2010. He estimated that manufacturing and other services in China's civil aviation industry reached ¥46.7 billion ($7.0 billion) during the five-year plan 2006–10 (China Business Review 2011). This will further increase global emissions as less advanced models enter the world fleet, including sales to airlines based outside China.

The infant aircraft industry in China may not be able to match the fuel efficiency of the advanced models from the established manufacturers, but they are likely to be competitive on price. Low-cost airlines will weigh up the cheaper purchase price against greater expenditure on fuel and, while fuel remains cheap, may decide that a less expensive, thirstier plane is the most economic option.

China and the developing world have a lot of catching up to do in the aspiration to match the developed world. This is understandable, and Western policy-makers have no grounds to deny them the opportunity. This massive expansion, and the associated environmental impact, is a problem for the whole world. Responsibility for the problem rests squarely with the developed world because this is where the model of low-cost flying was pioneered without understanding fully the consequences of rolling out such a model across world aviation. The developing world would be wrong to follow the same model, now that the dangers are evident, but it is reasonable for poorer nations to expect that the developed world lead the changes in aviation in parallel with poorer nations reining in their expectations.

The future of world aviation will be decided within the countries that lead the transition to sustainable policy. Leadership could come from any quarter, but morally it should come from the richer countries that have been emitting high levels of CO_2 for many years and where there are the resources to implement change. The core problem is not expansion in the developing world but the model of flying established by the richer countries.

Flying as a commodity

Flying has become a routine, reliable, standardized product. Passengers hardly notice the model of the aircraft or the underlying technology. The service is consumed without questioning how it is delivered. This lack of concern extends to the fumes coming out of the engines left behind in the slipstream. Unquestioning support for conventional aviation is making us blind to how it could be better. For business, virtual reality technology is entering videoconferencing so that it will become a credible substitute for face-to-face meetings. Many tourists are no longer curious adventurers but part of a mass movement of holidaymakers demanding that food and entertainment match closely what they have at home.

Aviation is firmly entrenched in a business-as-usual model with those operating the industry committing to continuing the expansion, supported by policy-makers not wanting to disrupt what they regard as a key industry. To understand the bind that aviation finds itself in requires an examination of the economic models that are universally applied.

The economics of the aviation industry

The economic models used by the aviation industry are as complex as the industry to which they are applied. It is also a very competitive industry in which commercial operators have little scope to give a high priority to environmental issues – and still remain in business.

Airline economists discuss issues such as economies of scale, the benefits of consolidating operations and the merits of the hub-and-spoke system in which passengers are flown into a large hub airport to catch a transfer flight to their final destination, allowing airlines to use fewer high-capacity planes but requiring passengers to change flights, except when travelling to or from the hub destination. It would be difficult to give a full account of the commercial and economic dynamics of the industry in just a few pages, so I will focus on the extent to which airline economics deals with the environmental impact of CO_2 emissions.

To write this section, three standard textbooks of airline economics were consulted. Two out of the three books made no mention of environmental factors: *Introduction to Air Transport Economics* (Vasigh et al. 2008) and *Flying Off Course: Airline Economics and Marketing* by Rigas Doganis (2010). The environment was not even listed in the index of these two books. An example of the advice offered is:

> Airlines can try to mitigate the impacts of high fuel prices at certain airports by reducing their fuel uplift at those airports to the minimum necessary. Instead, captains may be instructed to tanker as much fuel as possible at airports where fuel prices are low. Such a policy, however, needs careful monitoring since extra fuel will be burnt during the flight to carry the additional fuel loaded. This is because fuel consumption rises as the total weight of the aircraft increases. (Doganis 2010: 92)

Conventional economics is blind to the fact that to tanker fuel around the skies emits greater amounts of CO_2 than necessary. The advice from the economics textbook is that the decision is a trade-off between burning a lot of cheap fuel or a smaller quantity of more expensive fuel. If it costs less to burn a lot more cheap fuel, that is the most economic course of action. Such analysis is the reason that locks down tax-free aviation fuel throughout the industry. Airlines have the right to tanker in fuel and not to pay tax on it. Therefore any country that chose to lead in taxing aviation fuel would find foreign airlines tankering fuel to avoid refuelling while national airlines with their hubs in the country would be hit hard. This would be a spectacular own goal, so with few exceptions countries don't lead with raising tax on aviation fuel.

Decisions made by airlines are based on commercial grounds with a view to maximizing profit. For example, as airlines consider the purchase of cheaper models using less advanced technology from the emerging aircraft manufacturing industry in China, they will be calculating the total cost of ownership. These aircraft are likely to be less fuel efficient than the newest models from industry heavyweights Boeing and Airbus. Increased fuel consumption will have a greater impact on the calculation as oil prices rise, but if the initial purchase price is sufficiently cheap, the commercial decision will lean towards the least-cost solution, which could be the less fuel-efficient aircraft. Airlines are behaving as expected according to the textbooks, to maximize the return to their shareholders.

The third book I reviewed, *Straight and Level: Practical Airline Economics* by Stephen Holloway, has nine pages (out of 586) dedicated to 'Environmental Pressures'. This is largely a sound analysis and a useful insight into how the aviation industry sees itself and its performance with regard to environmental issues. The section that presents a snapshot of the current situation is the advice that Holloway provides the airline industry to communicate its environmental credentials. He suggests that the message that the industry should be putting out has six elements (Holloway 2008: 260):

- First, the industry contributes far more than most casual observers probably realise to the economic, social and cultural fabric of the planet ... any significant constraint placed on its growth would do serious economic and social harm without producing commensurate environmental benefits.
- Second, there is still only limited understanding of the true environmental impact of aviation ...
- Third, the industry has been taking its environmental responsibilities seriously for several decades ...
- Fourth, the practical results ... are evident in the fact that each new generation of transport aircraft is so much cleaner, quieter and fuel efficient than its predecessors ...

- Fifth, in some parts of the world politicians and other vested interests are standing in the way of further improvements in the industry's performance ... [referring to indirect routings and flight delays caused by inefficient air traffic management]
- Sixth, cattle generate twice as much greenhouse gas each year as do aircraft.

This view from inside the industry is interesting because the focus is on how to defend business-as-usual. A brief comment on each point is useful in exposing the disingenuous nature of the advice offered by Holloway. First, 'any significant constraint placed on its growth would do serious economic and social harm without producing commensurate environmental benefits'. In Chapters 7 and 15, I show that this is at best debatable and at worst plain wrong. Second, 'there is still only limited understanding of the true environmental impact of aviation ...'. There is very good understanding of the environmental impact of CO_2 emissions from aviation, although further work is needed to investigate the significance of the fact that high-altitude emissions (of CO_2 and other exhaust gases) have a greater impact than emissions at ground level. Third, 'the industry has been taking its environmental responsibilities seriously for several decades ...'. Looking at the slow progress towards migrating away from fossil fuels, this would indicate that the industry (or the politicians and regulators) has to significantly ramp up its efforts. Fourth, 'each new generation of transport aircraft is so much cleaner, quieter and fuel efficient than its predecessors ...'. This is progress but, interestingly, only the newest airliners just coming into service exceed the fuel-per-passenger-mile figures of the propeller-driven passenger aircraft of the 1950s on which aviation relied before the dawn of the jet age (discussed more fully in Chapter 11). Fifth, 'in some parts of the world politicians and other vested interests are standing in the way of further improvements in the industry's performance ...'. It is true that air traffic management needs to be improved and there are quick wins available here to reduce fuel burn through direct flights and less 'stacking' waiting to land.

Sixth, 'cattle generate twice as much greenhouse gas each year as do aircraft'. Industry chief executives would be wise not to use this excuse in public forums as it gives the impression that the industry is scrabbling for evidence in its defence.

Holloway also writes, with respect to the international agreements that prevent signatories from taxing fuel used by other parties' carriers for international service, 'The fear amongst airlines is that some governments might be inclined to break this 60-year practice to boost their environmental credentials' (ibid.: 327). The industry is living in denial by assuming that governments can be persuaded to maintain a sixty-year old rule to keep aviation fuel tax free. Textbooks would serve the industry rather better with a detailed analysis of how the economic models will change when this protection is lifted. It seems very odd that there is so little useful discussion. Perhaps there is a worry that to seriously discuss this outcome would be self-fulfilling.

Business flying

For business travellers, the aim is to make most productive use of the time spent in transit. For long-haul flights, seats that convert into beds have been introduced, allowing executives to get a good night's sleep and hit the ground ready to go straight to work. At destinations across the world there are hotels that are near identical. The experience can be as familiar and reassuring as if you had stayed at home, so workers are relaxed, productive and effective. Another way to achieve a similar outcome is not to fly.

Until recently, business travel was necessary because the alternatives to face-to-face meetings were limited. Now there are credible alternatives in advanced videoconferencing facilities that are morphing into full virtual reality systems. The eyeball-to-eyeball meeting, fully informed by all the subtle indicators of human interaction, and sealed with a real warm human handshake, will still be needed to close key negotiations, but most routine business meetings could take place within these advanced online virtual environments.

Leisure flying

Flying brings the benefit of opening up the world community, connecting people and cultures. To observe and experience another country is to learn; to learn is to understand; to understand is to prevent misunderstanding and defuse potential conflict. People who fly to observe, learn and experience, or act as an ambassador to communicate and teach, help to keep world society safe, but this applies to a small proportion of passengers, so the benefits of mass aviation to world society are fewer than is often supposed.

Many passengers are not looking for engagement with other cultures but simply want a holiday. This could be a place with antique shops, good restaurants and good wine, or simply sea, sun and cheap beer. The stereotype of British tourists in Spain is that they expect to speak English, want to eat British food and drink the same brands as in the pub back home. The attraction is reliable warm weather. Some exotic entertainment is welcome, as is a trip to a local historic site, provided the hotel or holiday complex has a familiar feel and satellite TV.

The decisions holidaymakers take are focused on securing the best deal. For a Londoner, if the prices of hotels on the Costa del Sol or in the south of France are too expensive, flights to Egypt or West Africa are other options. For a New Yorker bored with Florida, then it is just a few hours farther south to Cancún or Acapulco in Mexico, a favourite with the 1960s jet set. These are economic choices, with the flight costs one relatively small component.

A holiday on the other side of the planet used to be a rare once-in-a-lifetime experience. Now increasing numbers of people can afford to jet off in the summer and take a ski holiday in the winter, supplemented by flying off for a long weekend in the spring and autumn, to anywhere in the world, depending on the time available. Unemployment is not a barrier to jet-setting. Many regional flights are so cheap that people with flexibility as to when to fly can fly for next to nothing.

The new commuters

Cheap flying also supports new commuter profiles, according to a simple economic model. Work is available in place A but accommodation near by is expensive, or unattractive, or the kids don't want to move school. Place B is a cheap and/or pleasant place to live. Transport costs are an overhead that has to be factored in. While flying is cheap, commuter profiles that used not to be cost effective are now affordable.

A colleague working in a business school in the UK, not renowned for high salaries, commutes weekly to France. In France, he gets a better house than the expensive prices of southern England would allow and experiences the weather he prefers. Another example is a fireman I met who was weekly commuting between a job in the UK and his family living in Finland. These commuter profiles have a huge carbon footprint but, employing a purely financial perspective, the individuals involved do not have to factor that into their decisions.

From the viewpoint of an observer who understands the environmental impact of mass aviation, it seems wrong that the system of world aviation makes such lifestyle choices possible.

Air cargo

Air cargo is locked into traditional economic modelling even more than passenger flights. Flying is more expensive than sea or rail so is used for higher-value and perishable goods. Of course, there is more to it than a simple comparison between transport options. The decision must also take into account where to manufacture or grow produce. While air transportation is cheap, supply chains can extend halfway around the planet. When flying becomes significantly more expensive (an unavoidable consequence of effective sustainable policy), this will ripple through the world economy, bringing production back closer to the consumer. This would not be an attack on the world economy but a reconfiguration of the world economy. In the broader agenda of a more sustainable society this is a desirable outcome. It would not cause 'serious economic and social harm' – as the aviation economics textbooks would have us believe – but quite the reverse. The only harm will be to the airlines that have not anticipated that world society is capable of taking action in support of environmental outcomes and have therefore been caught unprepared.

Aviation locked in denial

The airline industry has matured into a global highly competitive industry. To airline bosses it is all about 'bums on seats'. To passengers it is all about the cheapest ticket price. Not many people will be aware of the model of plane, just the departure gate number and boarding time.

Passengers have become completely disconnected from the process of flying and flying has become disconnected from the needs of the environment. The atmosphere is no more than an external place in which exhaust gases can be dumped. Fortunately the atmosphere is rather big; so our particular flight does not matter. That sentiment is repeated for every one of the 7 million passengers who fly each day.[1]

Flying in the current generation of aeroplanes is like smoking. We now know that it is damaging to our long-term health but we persist. It would be better to kick the habit but we are hooked. The denial by a smoker that health problems may affect them is a personal choice. Denial that aviation is bad for the ecosystem is a deeply disturbing abjuration of responsibility. The argument over smoking has been won, with regulations that restrict smoking in public places and taxes applied to more than cover the extra costs to the public health system. In a similar way, conventional flying needs new regulations that include restrictions and taxes to at least cover the environmental impact. The logic is clear, but like the opposition that arose to restrictions on smoking, the challenge of implementing the logical solution should not be underestimated.

Adherence to market fundamentalism has laid the foundations for a massive expansion in the years ahead, but the basis of the

---

1 Based on IATA figures of 2.4 billion passengers annually (2009) rising to 2.75 billion in 2011.

market is flawed. In a tightly regulated industry, international regulations ensure that aviation fuel remains free of tax. Some proponents of laissez-faire capitalism rather like this situation, but it is a barrier to the reforms required to move beyond fossil fuel propulsion technology.

Aviation is a sector where emission reduction measures can be made easily. This statement will draw vociferous opposition from defenders of conventional aviation, who argue that it is hard to replace aviation fuel with renewable sources. They are missing the point; most flights are discretionary expenditure rather than a fundamental need. When world leaders become serious about tackling climate change, they will plan measures to constrain capacity for passengers and freight as well as change the economic parameters to support the development and deployment of a new generation of air vehicles with markedly less impact on the atmosphere. There may be regrets that the stalemate that grips the industry was not broken sooner to start the transformation towards greener aviation.

TWO | **Aviation today**

4 | Living the dream

There shall be wings! If the accomplishment be not for me, 'tis for some other.   Leonardo da Vinci (1452–1519)[1]

The age-old puzzle of how to fly was solved through the course of the twentieth century. People and air cargo now shuttle between airports in an expanding and increasingly complex network of routes. There has been astounding progress since the first sustained powered flight by the Wright brothers at Kitty Hawk in 1903. Their rudimentary flying machine used basic technology derived from bicycle engineering. Through the next 100 years, propellers gave way to jet engines and open cockpits were replaced by pressurized cabins. Almost exactly a century after that first flight, a team won the $10 million prize[2] for building the first commercial 'aircraft' to fly into space and back.

This chapter is an account of the development of aviation from the early beginnings through to the dawn of mass aviation and on to the current era of deregulation and rapid expansion. This rapid skim through history picks out the milestones that explain where aviation is today and indicates some of the lessons that must not be forgotten in looking to the future.

Dreaming of flying

The concept of flying has always held a special magical attraction for humans. To fly is a metaphor for freedom and success. Over the last century, for the first time in human history, people have been able to live the dream to fly.

---

1 Quoted in Merejkowski (1901).

2 The Ansari X PRIZE required that a private team build and launch a spacecraft capable of carrying three people to 100 kilometres above the Earth's surface, twice within two weeks (X PRIZE Foundation 2010).

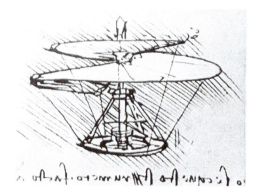

4.1 Da Vinci's
helicopter design

The concept that controlled manned flight might be possible goes back at least five hundred years to Leonardo da Vinci's sketch design for a heavier-than-air machine. It looked something like a primitive helicopter. He planned to use muscle power to revolve the rotor but human power could never have been enough to create sufficient lift. He needed a better power source. The missing ingredients were an engine and fuel to power it. It would be centuries before the discovery of oil and the invention of the internal combustion engine.

The helicopter proved to be a difficult technical challenge. French inventor Paul Cornu built the first free-flying piloted helicopter in 1907, but the design was unstable and was abandoned. It was not until the 1930s that the first true helicopters were developed by Focke-Wulf in Germany, with matching rotors spinning in opposite directions, and Sikorsky in the United States,

4.2 Focke-Wulf Fw 61

4.3 Sikorsky R4 Helicopter, 14 August 1944

who introduced the single rotor and a balancing tail rotor which would become the standard configuration.

Leonardo da Vinci would be astounded to see his sketch come to life in such dramatic fashion, and proud of human accomplishment. He would also be deeply frustrated that humans are doing so little to apply modern technology and new-found expertise to today's challenge of taking fossil fuels out of aviation. The pioneers of flying were able to take their ideas into the air because of oil, providing a huge boost to the development of flight. However, oil dependency has now become the problem that the pioneers of twenty-first-century flight will have to solve.

The innovative designers and engineers of today must be given the freedom to explore and experiment with novel low-carbon solutions following in the footsteps of da Vinci.

A lost opportunity – airships

Fixed-wing aircraft dominate modern aviation, but in the early years of flight, airships were thought to have considerable potential. One hundred years ago, British military authorities financed the development of airships in preference to aircraft because they could carry greater loads than aircraft. An airship pilot with the Royal Flying Corps in 1913 based at Farnborough in southern England recalled (Levine 2008: 16):

45

I was living about fourteen miles from Farnborough, where I was stationed, and one morning, I thought I'd go home for breakfast so I flew my airship over and circled around my house until the butler came out. He fetched the gardener. The two of them pulled me down and tied the airship to a tree at one end and a garden roller at the other. And I went in and had breakfast.

Airships seem like an old-fashioned concept from the distant past but, as demand for greener aviation grows, their ability to move heavy loads efficiently will be in demand once again. Modern airships have enormous potential to transport people and freight. The environmental benefit is the frugal use of fuel, although flying speed has to be low, in the region up to 130 mph, to achieve low fuel burn. Other benefits are high capacity, long range and ability to 'land' almost anywhere.

The most infamous airship of all time was the *Hindenburg*, leaving a negative image that endures to today. The German passenger airship LZ 129 *Hindenburg* left Frankfurt for Lakehurst, New Jersey, on 3 May 1937. It crossed the Atlantic and arrived three days later. Modern airships use the safe inert gas helium to provide buoyancy but the *Hindenburg* used the highly flammable gas hydrogen. After a delay of several hours, to avoid a line of thunderstorms, the *Hindenburg* attempted to dock with its mooring mast. It suddenly burst into flames and plunged to the ground. The moment was caught on film and remains a powerful and iconic image, effectively killing the concept of airships through the rest of the twentieth century.

The airship deserves to have its reputation restored. Its role may be limited by the lack of speed but it can do point-to-point journeys with precision and needs very little ground infrastructure. A century on, the technology is available to design and build advanced airships which may look very different to the airships of the past and be much more capable. This opportunity must not be missed again; modern airships will be an important component of the future green aviation transport network.

The dawn of mass aviation

Through the 1960s into the 1970s and beyond, air travel took over as the default option for international travel. First class and business class remained expensive but flying was no longer the preserve of the rich.

As a boy in the 1960s I travelled to Europe from Australia with my cost-conscious parents. We sailed on the P&O-Orient Lines ship *Orcades* from Sydney harbour, arriving at Tilbury Docks, London, five weeks later. This was just before aviation replaced the passenger liner as the low-cost choice for international travel. My overwhelming memory, from the viewpoint of a child, was a wonderful holiday cruise. I still have vivid memories of the ceremonies of crossing the Equator and looking out on Egypt from the handrail as we sailed through the Suez Canal (my mother, with four young children to look after, has more fraught memories). My father, an academic, used the time to write some chapters of the book he was working on.

As mass aviation took off, travel became much faster and more efficient from the perspective of the efficient use of people's time. Passenger ships are now used almost exclusively for cruising, which may entail taking a flight in order to reach the port of departure. From the viewpoint of sustainable policy this is wasteful. The world could learn to appreciate again the role of modern passenger liners, fitted with the latest sail and renewable energy propulsion technologies, and able to regain a sizeable chunk of the mass aviation market if flying was not so very cheap.

As aviation grew into a reliable worldwide network, it was seen as the future of international travel. More people could travel farther more often. Resources were diverted from developing more advanced shipping and better rail networks because these became less necessary.

Environmentalism emerges

The 1970s was the decade when environmentalism began to enter the political debate and aviation could have been set on a different path. The opportunity was wasted and aviation became ensnared in a policy trap which still grips the industry today.

In the United States, the emergence of a modern environmental movement in the 1960s was epitomized by the publication of *Silent Spring*, a book by Rachael Carson (1962) which catalogued the environmental impacts of the indiscriminate spraying of the pesticide DDT (Dunlap and Mertig 1992). She examined the effects on ecology, human health and wildlife, particularly birds. The concern this generated brought environmentalism to a wide audience, leading, in 1970, to the establishment of the United States Environmental Protection Agency (EPA).

Internationally, the United Nations Conference on the Human Environment held in Stockholm, Sweden, in June 1972 was the UN's first major conference on international environmental issues. This marked a turning point in the development of international environmental politics, leading to the setting up of the United Nations Environment Programme (UNEP).[3]

These actions in the early 1970s were the seeds that have grown into the discussion that continues today, about the role of human society in relation to the planet's ecosystem. Until very recently, aviation has remained aloof from the debate as a special case. Although it has been attacked vigorously by radical greens it has been defended strongly by government and policy-makers. In the 1970s, environmentalists found their voice but they did not make significant inroads into influencing the direction of aviation.

Four decades after environmentalism entered mainstream policy-making, it is no longer justifiable that aviation should remain a special case for exemption.

Deregulation

> I really don't know one plane from the other. To me they are just marginal costs with wings.   American economist Alfred Kahn, 1977

---

3 UNEP was founded by United Nations General Assembly Resolution 2997 (XXVII) of 15 December 1972.

From 1977 through 1978, American economist Alfred Kahn served as chairman of the US Civil Aeronautics Board (CAB), which regulated commercial airline fares. He made the comment quoted above during a meeting with airline executives who were trying to educate him about the merits of different aircraft (McCraw 1984). As an economist, Kahn was not going to be deflected. Under his leadership aviation became a commodity to be traded within a free market. He championed the Airline Deregulation Act of 1978, which among other actions disbanded the CAB six years later – a rare outcome of a regulator regulating itself out of existence. This opened the door to competition and set the framework for the emergence of the low-cost carriers.

Kahn's action laid the foundation for the expansion of modern aviation and set in place free-market disciplines that have been effective in a narrow economic context but have become a barrier to taking into account environmental factors. Looking forward, the challenge is to change policy to bring the environment inside the aviation policy framework.

The 1970s oil crisis

The 1970s oil crisis made the world pause and contemplate a future that was less dependent on oil. This could have been a turning point. Over the decades since the 1970s there have been a number of spikes in the price of oil, and numerous warnings that oil will one day run out, but none has been heeded. Aviation continues down a track that presupposes that oil will continue to be available and affordable.

The first oil crisis started in October 1973 when the Organization of the Petroleum Exporting Countries (OPEC) implemented steep price rises and an embargo on those countries that had supported Israel in the Yom Kippur war, notably the United States and the Netherlands. Supplies of oil to the UK were not affected as the UK had placed an embargo on arms and supplies to both the Israelis and the Arabs so did not draw retaliation from OPEC. However, the UK was hit hard by the combination of higher oil prices and a strike by UK coal miners through the winter of

1973/74. As supply was choked off, there was much talk of how to reduce reliance on oil.

Politicians and airlines considered their options. Airlines responded quickly by cancelling some flights and introducing fuel surcharges on ticket prices. A number of airlines also announced the retirement of their least fuel-efficient aircraft. These were first-generation jet airliners from the early 1950s that were coming to the end of their useful life. This was bringing forward a decision rather than planning a radical reconfiguration of their fleets. On 23 December 1973 the US president, Richard Nixon, decided to show his commitment to conserving fuel by flying as a passenger aboard a United Airlines DC-10 flight from Washington Dulles to Los Angeles instead of using Air Force One. In keeping with the common practice an Air Force aircraft flew behind in case of an emergency. In terms of an immediate response, there was not much more that could be done. Planning a transport system that is less dependent on oil requires long-term strategic planning. Designing and building new aircraft, or enhancing other transport options, takes time and investment.

The 1970s oil crisis was soon resolved, with the embargo lifted after five months. Relatively high prices remained, but OPEC members took a more conciliatory approach and avoided further abrupt price increases. I suspect one issue that influenced OPEC was the response of the West to the oil crisis. OPEC may have seen evidence that if they pushed too hard then the West could choose to break its reliance on oil. OPEC has behaved responsibly over the decades since the 1970s, ensuring that oil remains affordable, and often increasing production in response to higher prices. The West became less concerned about oil supplies and less interested in investing in alternatives.

At the time of the 1970s oil crisis, the strategic decision to be less reliant on oil could have been made, backtracking on fossil-fuel dependency. Replacing an infrastructure predicated on oil, if undertaken on a rolling basis when renewal becomes due, would take many decades. The three decades from that era to today would have been the sort of timescale needed. It is a shame that the opportunity was squandered, but it is not surprising. The situation the world faced in the 1970s was different. Although the dangers of reliance on oil from regions beyond a government's control were plain, the full impact on the environment of burning fossil fuel was not widely understood.

The 1980s and beyond – return to business as usual

The year 1986 was a milestone in aviation history when the super-efficient *Voyager* aeroplane completed a non-stop circumnavigation of the globe. The first non-stop flight with in-flight refuelling had been completed by the US Air Force in 1949, but the significance of *Voyager* was that it completed the record-breaking flight without refuelling. *Voyager* was built from graphite composites with careful design so that its drag was lower than that of almost any other powered aircraft.

On 14 December 1986 the *Voyager* took off from Edwards Air Force Base, California, with so much fuel on board that the wing-tips dragged on the ground, sustaining minor damage. Just over nine days later it returned (Figure 4.4) to land back at Edwards. The significance of this flight was the emphasis on super-efficient aerodynamics – an important lesson for green aviation.

Unfortunately the political climate of the 1980s under the Reagan presidency was not conducive to building on the technical success of *Voyager*. According to the American author Richard Heinberg, the Reagan message was that 'the people of the US

4.4 The *Voyager* aircraft

should forget their worries about energy-resource limits and return to their proper pastimes – spending, driving and wasting'. In a highly symbolical act, Reagan ordered that the solar hot-water panels installed on the White House by President Jimmy Carter be removed (Heinberg 2005).

During the Reagan presidency (1981–89) there was not just indifference to environmental issues but efforts to roll back existing environmental regulations. President Clinton and Vice-President Gore (1993–2001) offered the hope of change, coming into office committed to demonstrating that a strong economy and a clean environment go hand in hand. Despite bringing an environmental conscience back into the White House, the Clinton presidency met resistance and made little substantive progress. The arrival of George W. Bush (2001–09) ended any hope of substantive action on environmental issues. He will be remembered for his withdrawal of United States support from the then-pending Kyoto Protocol in his first year in office. With politics such as this, right at the very top of world political leadership, there was little chance that aviation could be deflected on to a greener path. The industry would have to accept that business-as-usual was the order of the day and stick with an international regulatory regime that prevents progress towards sustainable aviation.

Addicted to oil

It seemed that world economies were at risk when the price of oil more than doubled as a result of the 1973/74 oil crisis. In 1979/80, as problems erupted in Iran, the second oil crisis hit with the oil price breaking $37 a barrel ($97 at 2009 prices). During the 1980s and 1990s the price eased back, lulling the world into a false sense of security, dropping to under $15 ($29) in 1986. In May 2008 steep price rises returned with the price for a barrel of oil exceeding $147 for the first time. Again, despite the protestations, the world economy took these rises in its stride (the financial problems that came later in 2008 were not blamed on the price of oil). The world is finding that economies can live with high oil prices. The next step is to discover whether the world economy can survive without oil.

Coming off oil dependency by free choice is a leap too far for many policy-makers. I argue that this can be done, and that economies will adjust to fit. Looking past short-term economics, as the British economist Nicholas Stern did in his report on climate change (2007), it can be seen that the long-term economic argument supports acting sooner rather than later.

The short-term vested interests of the oil companies and oil-rich nations will have to be overcome. These are very powerful lobbies; while the world remains focused on short-term economics, political leaders will listen to them.

Living the dream

5 | Progress out of crisis

The history of aviation has been punctuated by crisis events that have brought step-change in aviation. At the micro scale, each time an aircraft crashes there is an investigation that leads to a small step forward, such as redesigning an aircraft component or changing operating procedures. At the macro scale, the struggle and hardship of both world wars brought out innovation, pushing technology to new limits and stimulating huge leaps forward, providing the circumstances for aviation to flourish in the immediate aftermath.

There were two golden ages of aviation during the twentieth century. The first was the period after the First World War, in which flying became glamorous. Dashing young pilots competed for lucrative prize-money to be first to fly the big challenges such as transatlantic and round-the-world flights. The second golden age was the period following the Second World War (WW2) when the jet engine, designed in the search for speed in fighter aircraft, led to commercial jet airliners. Both these golden ages were driven by post-war euphoria and the availability of inexpensive surplus military aircraft.

In this chapter it is observed that each golden age has been initiated by developments arising out of crisis. Later chapters will look forward to another golden age arising out of changes in policy and technological advances in response to increasing concerns over climate change.

The second golden age of aviation

The post-war years after WW2 were a time to rebuild damaged infrastructure and to rebuild society. There was optimism and hope for the future. Politicians planned a new world order in which aviation would play an important role. Favourable regulations were put in place to encourage growth and expansion which are still in place today. For the airlines, there were ample numbers of ex-military aircraft to start building their fleets. In aircraft and infrastructure design there were wartime technologies to exploit, such as radar and the jet engine. The circumstances were ripe for aviation to boom.

After the war, there was no market for surplus fast fighter aircraft, but the glut of heavy bomber airframes like those of the B-29 and Lancaster were useful and could be converted into commercial aircraft. The most successful demobilized aircraft was the C-47, a military version of the Douglas DC-3, used for troop carrying and cargo. Thousands of these, previously operated by several air forces, were converted for civilian use after the war and became the standard equipment of almost all the world's airlines. They were large and fast by the standards of the day. The ready availability of these cheap, easily maintained ex-military aircraft underpinned the initial expansion of the post-war air transport industry.

Setting priorities During the war, aviation developed according to military priorities. These included the delivery of supplies, ferrying troops, transporting casualties and the key task of keeping control of the airspace. For this prime task the need was for speed. A fighter aircraft needs agility but first and foremost it must be fast; all other requirements are secondary. After the war, the technology of fighters became available for civil aviation, in particular the jet engine, developed in the closing stages of the war in the search for yet more speed.

When airships were in their heyday it took three days to cross the Atlantic. This was reduced to sixteen hours with propeller-driven aircraft. When jet-powered planes entered passenger service this was halved to around eight hours.

The model of airline operations post-war was an exclusive service at relatively high cost. It was not envisaged that flying would become so universal and cheap that people across society would become passengers. Passengers were the relatively better off or business people who had to travel. Flying was a special and, for most ordinary people, a rare experience.

Post-war aviation was small in scale; the idea that environmental factors might be important was overlooked. The Earth has a huge atmosphere; the pollution pumped into it is soon dispersed, especially if the emissions were at high altitude and out of sight and out of mind.

Cold War The rivalry between the Western powers and the Soviet Union shaped the post-war era. Again, developments in aviation were driven by military needs. The search for speed continued with the secret US research plane code-named the X-1, the forerunner of supersonic fighter intercept aircraft, described as a 'bullet with wings' and the first plane to break the sound barrier in level flight, a feat achieved in 1947 (Yeager et al. 1997).

The search for speed increased fuel burn, but this was not a factor that concerned military aero engineers. Their designs for interceptor aircraft might have been needed to fight a third world war; fuel efficiency was not important. The Cold War also required surveillance aircraft able to operate for long periods at high altitude. The U-2 spy plane resulted from a well-funded secret military project to design an aircraft to fly continuously on the edge of space at an altitude of 70,000 feet. Developed initially for the CIA, later models are still in service, flying reconnaissance missions over Afghanistan. The U-2 came out of the shadows when one was shot down over the USSR in 1960 and the pilot, Francis Gary Powers, captured. It came to prominence again in 1962 when a U-2 was shot down over Cuba during the Cuban missile crisis.

The long wings of the U-2 allow it to fly efficiently and very high. At these rarefied altitudes the aircraft flies within a very narrow flight envelope[1] nicknamed 'coffin corner' by aviators. Any slower and the aircraft will stall; any faster and the critical Mach number at which lift can be lost owing to flow separation and shock waves

---

1 The 'flight envelope' for an aircraft is the range of flying parameters with which it can cope.

will be exceeded. To maintain the high altitude needed to avoid interception the pilot is flying with very little margin for error.

The super-efficient glider characteristics of the U-2 will be needed in the third golden age of aviation when fuel efficiency will be paramount, flying at lower altitude within a safe performance envelope away from coffin corner.

Beyond the atmosphere The final frontier in aviation was to leave the confines of the atmosphere and 'fly' in space. The Soviet Union were first, putting Yuri Gagarin into orbit for 108 minutes in his *Vostok 1* spacecraft on 12 April 1961. The United States sought to regain the lead and embarked upon an even greater challenge. Within weeks of Yuri Gagarin's flight, President Kennedy announced in a speech to a joint session of Congress on 25 May 1961: 'I believe that this nation should commit itself to achieving the goal, before this decade is out, of landing a man on the Moon and returning him safely to Earth.'

The second golden age of aviation reached its pinnacle in 1969, when *Apollo 11* landed on the moon and Neil Armstrong, as he stepped out, said the famous words 'That's one small step for man, one giant leap for mankind'. From the Cold War defeat, of losing the race into space, the United States rose to the challenge to win the next challenge of reaching the moon. President Kennedy's pledge was fulfilled in just eight years from presidential vision to delivery. This shows what can be achieved within a short time frame where there is strong and clear political leadership. The third golden age, based on minimizing the environmental impact of flying, could be delivered in a comparable timescale if politicians showed similar vision and resolve.

Onward to the third golden age of aviation

If circumstances change, such that society believes that catastrophic climate change is a real possibility, then bold and decisive action becomes possible.

There are lessons to learn from the golden ages of the past to help guide developments of the future.

Act quickly During WW2, the scope and speed with which the Allies responded was astounding. In Britain, a massive programme of aircraft-building and airfield construction was initiated. For example, Greenham Common near Newbury in southern England was identified as a site for an airfield. An Air Ministry requisition was issued in March 1941 and the common, together with a part of Crookham Common, was acquired two months later. Crookham Golf Club on the north side of the base was also taken over, with the final round played before the end of 1941.

Compare this with the ten years it took to get planning permission for the Whitelee wind farm, which, at the time of writing, is Europe's largest onshore wind farm (Power-technology 2010). The site has 140 turbines, which can generate 322 Mw of electricity, enough to power 180,000 homes. It is an award-winning showpiece of renewable energy technology (Scottish Green Energy Awards 2009). The location, on windswept Eaglesham Moor, is just 15 kilometres from the energy-hungry city of Glasgow and a perfect site for a wind farm. There was a decade of discussion between identification of the site in 1999 and commissioning the wind farm in May 2009. WW2 could have been fought from beginning to end, twice, in the time it took to bring 322 Mw of renewable energy into operation.

In the summer of 1942, a little over one year from identifying the site, Greenham Common airfield was ready to receive the US 51st Troop Carrier Wing. One hundred and twenty aircraft flew in hops across the Atlantic from Massachusetts via Goose Bay, Labrador, Greenland, Iceland and then Prestwick airport in Scotland. This is a short distance to the south-west of Eaglesham Moor, where Whitelee wind farm now sits. The 120 aircraft would still have been parked up there when WW2 ended if their destination airfield had been built to the time frame of a twenty-first-century renewable energy project. But this was war and their new base at Greenham Common was ready; the planes resumed their journey and flew south.

The land for Greenham Common was seized and the airfield constructed, to be operational in a little over one year. After the war it continued to operate as a Cold War bomber base with one of the longest runways in Europe. Only recently, the airfield was decommissioned and the land returned to the community.

The pace, ambition and innovation of the war effort would be hard to replicate today. This astonishing progress in technology from airframes and engines to computers and radar came about because the future of the country was at stake. The incentive to act and succeed could not have been stronger. The challenge is to find the determination to be equally bold in response to the dangers of climate change.

A sense of urgency If the world community accepted the impending environmental crisis as a threat to human society, acting within a five-year timescale would be feasible. The long-term targets that are discussed by politicians seem like a politically convenient fabrication. Setting a target for 2050 is simply kicking the issues out into the long grass, thus avoiding the need to expend political capital on making real progress. The year 2020 is a closer target, but this still allows WW2 to be fought from beginning to end with years to spare. If the risks to the environment really matter, the focus should be on what can be done within the next five years.

6 | The Chicago Convention

In 1943, as war was still raging in Europe, the USA initiated studies of post-war civil aviation. The US view was that civil aviation could be used as one of the principal elements in the economic development of the world and the first available means to start, in the words of President Roosevelt, 'healing the wounds of war' (ICAO 2010a).

The post-war vision of greater cooperation and improved governance under the auspices of the United Nations also included improved international transportation. It was recognized that a world in which communication is difficult and slow, and where people live isolated lives, can be a dangerous world. Rules and regulations to improve communications and facilitate trade between nations were seen as key components of building a prosperous and secure post-war world society. The new rules for civil aviation and new procedures for world governance were part of one agenda.

In this chapter, the pivotal role of the Convention on International Civil Aviation is examined, showing that it was appropriate to the challenges of its time when agreed in Chicago in 1944, but now its provisions are outdated, particularly the rules that ensure that aviation fuel is free of tax. Priorities have changed and it is time for a new convention on civil aviation to introduce significant taxation of aviation fuel.

The International Civil Aviation Conference

At the Anglo-American Conference, hosted by Canada in Quebec City from 10 to 24 August 1943, Roosevelt and Churchill discussed post-war aviation policy. They planned a multinational organization, following the model of the United Nations, to handle international civil aviation. On 11 September 1944, the United

States extended an invitation to fifty-three governments and two ministers (Danish and Thai) in Washington for an international civil aviation conference to be convened in the United States on 1 November 1944, 'to make arrangements for the immediate establishment of provisional world air routes and services ... and to discuss the principles and methods to be followed in the adoption of a new aviation convention' (ICAO 2010b).

Stevens Hotel in Chicago, Illinois, was chosen as the site for the International Civil Aviation Conference. A three-week meeting was anticipated but it took over five weeks for delegates to conclude an agreement. The result was the Convention on International Civil Aviation, referred to as the Chicago Convention. The preamble to the convention makes clear the intention of the governments to 'help to create and preserve friendship and understanding among the nations and peoples of the world ... and to promote that co-operation between nations and peoples upon which the peace of the world depends' (See Box 6.1).

Box 6.1 Preamble to the Convention on International
Civil Aviation (ICAO 2006)

Whereas the future development of international civil aviation can greatly help to create and preserve friendship and understanding among the nations and peoples of the world, yet its abuse can become a threat to the general security; and

Whereas it is desirable to avoid friction and to promote that co-operation between nations and peoples upon which the peace of the world depends;

Therefore, the undersigned governments having agreed on certain principles and arrangements in order that international civil aviation may be developed in a safe and orderly manner and that international air transport services may be established on the basis of equality of opportunity and operated soundly and economically;

Have accordingly concluded this Convention to that end.

As hosts, the USA wielded a strong influence, supporting technical regulations but wanting maximum economic freedom to operate. At a time when other countries were weak, the USA took the opportunity to put their stamp on the rules of aviation which endures to today.

The Convention on International Civil Aviation was signed on 7 December 1944 by fifty-two signatory states (the Soviet Union had been invited but did not attend and ratified the Convention only later in 1970). The Convention establishes rules of airspace, aircraft registration and safety, and details the rights of the signatories in relation to air travel. It also established the International Civil Aviation Organization (ICAO), a specialized agency of the United Nations charged with coordinating and regulating international air travel.

The Chicago Convention has since been revised eight times (in 1959, 1963, 1969, 1975, 1980, 1997, 2000 and 2006). These revisions are not major departures from the principles enshrined in the original agreement. The Chicago Convention remains the foundation of civil aviation and ensures that the industry is firmly locked into the post-war vision of the politicians of the 1940s.

Not surprisingly, aspects of this agreement are no longer appropriate for aviation in the twenty-first century. Article 24 states:

Fuel, lubricating oils, spare parts, regular equipment and aircraft stores on board an aircraft of a contracting State, on arrival in the territory of another contracting State and retained on board on leaving the territory of that State, shall be exempt from customs duty, inspection fees or similar national or local duties and charges.

This article has ensured that aviation fuel for international flights is universally exempt from tax. If one country were to take a national decision to tax aviation fuel, airlines would be within their rights to fly into that country with full tanks and avoid purchasing fuel. The outcome would be that more aviation fuel would be burnt – meaning more CO_2 emitted – as airlines tanker fuel from low-tax to high-tax locations. Such action would hit hardest those airlines with operating hubs in the country imposing the tax. Unilateral action would be an economic and environmental own goal. The result is stalemate, keeping aviation fuel artificially cheap.

The Chicago Convention has served its purpose for over sixty-five years, but the world has changed and priorities change. The Chicago Convention has become a barrier to progress and will need to be renegotiated or replaced. With such a large number of countries involved it will be difficult, but this is the nettle that will have to be grasped.

Altered priorities

As post-war aviation shrank the world, it provided the communications to improve cooperation and understanding between nations and a means to expand trade. Through the course of the twentieth century, the post-war vision of aviation becoming a force for the development of a more prosperous world seemed to be right.

In the twenty-first century, priorities have changed. The Chicago Convention locks down an outdated policy framework that prevents evolution to a greener aviation industry, keeping aviation fuel too cheap to justify designing and building the new generation of green air vehicles. The trigger to break the stalemate is to introduce taxation on aviation fuel, at an appropriate level to support the changes required.

General taxation on aviation is inefficiently low as a result of tax competition between countries defending domestic carriers and/or tourist sectors (Keen and Strand 2006). The tax exemption for aviation fuel, written into Article 24 of the Chicago Convention, is a particular concern. This provision was further reinforced by a resolution of the Council of the ICAO in 1999, stating that in addition to exemption from taxation of fuel on board an aircraft on arrival, 'it is the common practice of many States with respect to aircraft engaged in international transport generally to exempt from or refund taxes on fuel ... taken on board at the final airport in that customs territory' before departing the country (ICAO 2000).

Changing the status quo would be straightforward, from an

administrative perspective, because the supply system and the airports where planes refuel are tightly controlled. As with any tax, those who have to pay it, the airlines, will complain, but this is unlikely to earn much sympathy when it highlights the privileged tax-free status that airlines have enjoyed up to this point. In Europe, the cost of filling a car with fuel in London is nearly triple the price paid by an airline refuelling at Heathrow.[1] Introducing aviation fuel tax in the UK will do no more than remove this anomaly. In other countries, particularly the United States, it will be politically difficult.

Once the principle of an aviation fuel tax is established, the tax rate will become subject to heated political debate. Suggesting that it will cost more to fly – perhaps much more – is hard to do without raising people's hackles. Passengers will need convincing that their short-term expectations have to be reined in to initiate the third golden age of aviation in which environmental responsibility is central.

Resistance to taxing aviation fuel

Resistance to the introduction of an aviation fuel tax is likely to be strongest in the rich countries among people whose lifestyle is most dependent on affordable flights. A study by the UK Civil Aviation Authority found that the individuals who fly most often are from households with an annual income of over £115,000 and who own a home abroad (CAA 2008). This group take an average of over five return leisure flights per year. This is a lifestyle choice that they have made. As soon as it becomes clear that society will act on aviation, these people will reconsider their property ownership and lifestyle choices.

In rich countries, the people who may suffer most are those of modest means who have retired to sunny climes in the expectation of flying back at regular intervals to see the grandchildren. More expensive flights will mean they cannot afford to travel as often.

---

1 In February 2011 the cost of aviation fuel was much the same across all world markets, averaging around 75 cents per litre (IATA 2011); the cost of car fuel in London averaged around £1.30 ($2.11) per litre.

Their sons and daughters, with young families, may not be able to afford to visit. Cheaper property in remote sunny locations may drop in value as demand reduces, trapping the less well off in retirement enclaves cut off from family. They deserve sympathy, but the required action is not to defend cheap flights but to discourage potentially vulnerable people from buying retirement properties a long way from their home roots.

Popular support for greener aviation will follow in due course, but rich-world politicians will have to make a start by taking the lead. The issue of fairness will be crucial. Hypothecating the tax receipts to invest in greener transportation may be required to make action politically acceptable. The tax on aviation fuel will apply mainly to the richer people in society who are frequent flyers. Poorer people, who can no longer afford to fly, will object less when the rich are seen to pay a high price and investment is seen to flow into improved ground transport infrastructure appropriate to the needs of the general population.

Impact on the aviation industry

> In Europe we are fighting to regain leadership on the debate
> [about environmental taxes]. Politicians are building their
> green credentials at our expense. Giovanni Bisignani, director
> general, IATA (Bisignani 2007)

The aviation industry faces uncertain, challenging and exciting times. On one hand, conventional flying is incredibly cheap and good value (if the environmental impact is ignored), leading to continued growth in capacity. On the other hand, the aviation industry is facing the prospect of increased taxation as politicians, led by those in Europe, start to bring the industry into the twenty-first century.

The economics of flying will change. Each seat on a scheduled flight is a revenue-earning opportunity up until the time of departure. Forward bookings are cash in the bank with an unsold seat worthless as soon as the flight has departed. The primary expenses are fuel, staff and the capital costs of the aircraft –

incurred directly or as a payment under a lease agreement. When aviation fuel tax is introduced and increased sufficiently to support the transition, many seats will remain empty, capacity will be withdrawn and older conventional aircraft will become surplus and worth very little. This is the correct outcome to get to grips with sustainable aviation policy.

The transformation will seem to be a terminal decline at first with many existing airlines failing to survive the shake-out. Later, new commercial entities will rise up, owning the most valuable landing slots and the most efficient aircraft. The entrepreneurs working on designs for green air vehicles will push quickly towards building production models. The transition that might have taken the next twenty years could take place in five.

The strength of the resurgence in aviation will be proportional to the depth of the collapse. This will depend on the seriousness with which the risks of climate change are viewed. It is necessary to dismantle the old to rebuild the new within a short timescale.

Governments will be under pressure to rescue the industry. Care will be needed to support only those parts that need to survive. The United States and Europe may consider protecting the production lines of Boeing and Airbus but this will be difficult, because in a contracting market, with surplus aircraft, airlines will be able to buy older aircraft very cheaply and, despite high fuel costs, operate them at a profit. It might be tough to find capital for new aircraft even if they are more efficient. Governments could bring in cash-for-guzzlers programmes to pay towards purchasing a new Airbus A380 or Boeing 787 aircraft, provided older aircraft are scrapped and removed permanently from the world fleet. This would have similarities to the cash-for-clunkers programme used in America and Europe to support the car industry during the 2009 recession. Airbus and Boeing would then be under pressure to move quickly into the green air vehicle market as such incentives are withdrawn.

Renegotiating the Chicago Convention

Membership of the Chicago Convention has grown to 190 states. It is administered by the International Civil Aviation Organization (ICAO) with a General Assembly held triennially where the members of the Council are elected and major decisions taken. At the 37th ICAO General Assembly in October 2010, aviation and climate change were discussed. The final summing up of the agenda item on climate change includes commitments to further analysis and monitoring (ICAO 2010c). It concludes that the ICAO should define 'global solutions that will be applicable to all, based on the principles and provisions of the Chicago Convention'. It also states that the 'emphasis should be on those policy options that will reduce aircraft engine emissions without negatively impacting the growth of air transport especially in developing economies'.

The ICAO is resolutely defending the Chicago Convention and continued growth of air transport. It is inherently incompatible to seek to grow aviation, reduce carbon emissions and maintain tax-free fuel. This odd stance limits the scope for effective and ambitious action. It is the Chicago Convention which is now the policy block that has to be overcome. Instead of negotiating around the Convention, world leaders need to find the courage to confront its provisions. The Chicago Convention was conceived in time of crisis; it should be renegotiated as a response to the climate crisis.

Fundamental change could take place only at a General Assembly (held every three years) and would require a two-thirds majority. Article 94 states: 'Any proposed amendment to this Convention must be approved by a two-thirds vote of the Assembly and ... ratified by not less than two-thirds of the total number of contracting States.' Orchestrating change often starts with a proposal from the Council of the ICAO, which consists of representatives from thirty-six contracting states elected at the General Assembly to serve for three years. The proposal is discussed at the General Assembly and voted on. If passed, the proposal goes forward for ratification by the contracting states. This can drag on for many years until the required two-thirds majority is achieved. This ponderous process introduces required amendments to develop the policy framework but ensures that significant and rapid change to the core policy framework, particularly if it might be contentious, is practically impossible through this route.

The heritage and history of the Convention indicates another way. The world could adopt the can-do spirit in which the Convention was born. Assuming a number of pre-meetings to undertake the essential groundwork, it should be possible to replace the Convention with a climate-friendly agreement within the timescale that it was first drafted, five weeks. This would not happen under the auspices of the ICAO. The ICAO is tasked with administrating the Convention and naturally defends the status quo. The member states would have to lead the renegotiation, the most powerful of which is the United States. The pivotal role of the United States is illustrated by the procedure should a state wish to withdraw from the Convention. Article 95 states: 'Any contracting State may give notice of denunciation of this Convention ... by notification addressed to the Government of the United States of America.'

There have been calls to reform the Convention. In 2008, the UK Parliament called on the government to 'urgently seek reform of the Chicago Convention'. The Environmental Audit Committee urged that the 'Government seek the support of the new US Administration in promoting reform of the Chicago Convention to allow governments to impose a tax on international aviation fuel' (House of Commons 2008).

Despite these calls for action, there is little appetite for renegotiation of the Chicago Convention; so, the stalemate continues.

Unilateral action

Coordinated global action to trigger change would be difficult. Another route to consider is for countries to act alone. The UK government, listening to the environmentalists in Parliament, could decide to take unilateral action and tax aviation fuel in the UK. There are no regulations or rules to prevent Britain taking this national decision. However, the outcome would not be welcomed by the government, or environmentalists.

Any aircraft fuelling in the UK would pay the tax. The airlines would arrange their refuelling schedules to minimize the fuel taken on board in the UK. Foreign airlines would fly in with enough fuel on board for their next leg, unless this exceeded the capacity of their tanks. The short-haul flights to other European capitals would not need to refuel in the UK. UK-based airlines would suffer a huge commercial disadvantage unless they could change their schedules to take on most of the fuel they need while outside the UK. It would become cheaper to fly long-haul out of other European capitals. As airlines responded, London Heathrow would no longer be a major international hub. The economics would encourage passengers to enter Europe through airports in other European countries. Heathrow would become predominantly a short-haul destination. The politicians, and their advisers, can see this outcome, so a developed country like the UK is not going to take unilateral action to impose a significant tax on aviation fuel.

At the other end of the scale, let us consider a small developing country taking unilateral action. The low-lying Maldives have good reason to worry about climate change and support measures to reduce CO_2 emissions. President Mohamed Nasheed has spoken up in favour of tough targets to limit carbon emissions. The country aims to do what it preaches with a target of carbon neutrality by 2020. There is a lot that can be done to replace fossil fuel with solar power in these sun-drenched atolls. The reliable sunshine also makes the Maldives a major tourist destination, and tourism is the prime source of its foreign income. Zero carbon, a higher standard than carbon neutrality, would require that all tourists arrived on green sailing ships or on new-generation green air vehicles. This is the future to aim for, but in the near term carbon neutrality could be claimed through either leaving out the carbon footprint of the transport used by tourists to and from the islands, or offsetting it by paying for carbon-reduction projects in other countries. The Maldives also has the option of taking unilateral action to tax aviation fuel. Not only would the airlines depart for the islands with full tanks to minimize the fuel they purchase, but if other holiday resorts do not follow, the Maldives could kill its tourist economy.

Countries that depend on international tourism will not lead in taking unilateral action. Countries that have airlines based in their territories will not take unilateral action. Countries with aircraft manufacturing industries will not take unilateral action. The stalemate continues.

7 | Globalization and aviation

Air transport is critical to the fabric of the global economy, playing a critical role in wealth generation and poverty reduction. The livelihoods of 32 million people are tied to aviation, accounting for US$3.5 trillion in economic activity.   Giovanni Bisignani, director general, IATA (IATA 2007)

Globalization[1] has been the dominant theme of economic policy for the last three decades, promoting increased integration of economies, free trade and deregulation, but the policies of sustainability are rising up the policy agenda. Discrepancies between these two policy frameworks are starting to appear. The conventional view of globalization is that it requires high-capacity, affordable transportation. As sustainability becomes more important, policy will adjust to a new framework in which the role of aviation is less critical.

The dependency of the globalized economy on high-capacity affordable aviation is a key barrier to changing the international policy framework. To reform aviation is seen as an attack on the economy. The assumption that conventional aviation must be allowed to expand without fundamental reform, because the global economy demands it, is right at the heart of the argument. This assumption needs to be questioned and debated, not accepted blindly.

In this chapter, the interdependencies between globalization and aviation are examined, ranging from its role in facilitating trade to poverty reduction and tourism. It is argued that the time has come to rethink the policies of globalization in the context of sustainability, leading to the conclusion that there is no reason

---

1 'Globalization' in this chapter is synonymous with 'economic globalization'.

for special exemption for aviation from sound environmental regulations.

Globalization and sustainability

Sustainability came to the fore when the United Nations established the World Commission on Environment and Development (WCED) in 1983. The report from the Commission, *Our Common Future* (WCED 1987), often known as the Brundtland report after the chair, Gro Harlem Brundtland, considered questions about development, poverty reduction and environmentalism, showing that these issues were connected and indivisible. This was a profound insight which laid the foundations for developing the concepts of sustainable policy. Other significant milestones were the Earth Summit[2] of 1992, the United Nations Framework Convention on Climate Change (UNFCCC) of 1994 and the World Summit on Sustainable Development (WSSD)[3] of 2002. In recent years, a focus of sustainability has become controlling carbon emissions to avert the worst consequences of climate change. The protracted negotiations as world leaders try to agree robust measures to address climate change are a sign that the world is not yet ready to embrace the requirements of sustainability.

A key analysis that does not get the attention it deserves is the Millennium Ecosystem Assessment (2005). In 2000, the UN secretary general, Kofi Annan, called for an assessment of the world ecosystem. The Millennium Ecosystem Assessment, published in 2005, is one of the most important environmental reports ever produced and makes disturbing reading:

> Over the past 50 years, humans have changed these ecosystems more rapidly and extensively than in any comparable period of time in human history, largely to meet rapidly growing demands for food, fresh water, timber, fiber, and fuel. This

2 United Nations Conference on Environment and Development (UNCED) held in Rio de Janeiro, Brazil, 3–14 June 1992.

3 World Summit on Sustainable Development (WSSD) held in Johannesburg, South Africa, 26 August–4 September 2002.

transformation of the planet has contributed to substantial net gains in human well-being and economic development. But not all regions and groups of people have benefited from this process – in fact, many have been harmed. Moreover, the full costs associated with these gains are only now becoming apparent.

The Millennium Ecosystem Assessment should have initiated a debate about changing the way society and the economy operate to prevent long-lasting damage to the ecosystem. There has been a debate, and the debate continues, but it is among environmentalists who agree that something must be done. The debate should be drawing in economists and world leaders to discuss what that 'something' is in terms of real policy choices.

It is not widely understood or accepted that there are inherent incompatibilities between the policies of economic globalization and sustainability. Proponents of globalization in the richer countries are not yet ready to accept that market fundamentalism has its limits. They have support from people in the development community and some environmentalists, who believe that sustainability can be achieved through open interconnected markets. This is a delusion that will take some time to shift.[4] Global cooperation is of course important, but real robust solutions are to be found in supporting local, national and regional solutions, in that order of priority, in preference to adhering to the paradigm of globalization.

Reconciling the two agendas of 'globalization' and 'sustainability' has not received much attention. Economic policy continues to be dominated by the policies of globalization as championed by the IMF, the World Bank and the WTO. Officials at UNEP pursue an environmental agenda but the linkages across to economic policy are weak. The Economics and Trade Branch of the Division of Technology, Industry and Economics at UNEP is a small team. Their recent report, 'Green economy' (Sukhdev and Stone 2010), presents an interesting analysis that deserves to be debated widely,

4 The full argument for a real-world analysis of a greener world economy can be found in McManners (2010).

but it is unlikely that well-thumbed copies are to be found on the desks of officials in the IMF or WTO.

The political context

There should be considerable cross-fertilization between environmental and economic policy, but so far the linkages are few, not well known and not well understood. These important policy areas collide when world leaders gather to sign agreements drafted by their officials in the distinct areas of economics and environmental policy. The economists and environmental policy-makers are different groups of officials – and one has more power than the other.

President Obama, speaking to a bipartisan group of US governors on 18 November 2008 after he was elected but before he took office, was determined that the United States would take action over climate change:

> Now is the time to confront this challenge once and for all. Delay is no longer an option. Denial is no longer an acceptable response. The stakes are too high; the consequences too serious. Stopping climate change won't be easy and it won't happen overnight. But I promise you this: When I am President ... any nation that's willing to join the cause of combating climate change will have an ally in the United States of America.

President Obama found that, once he was in office, his ability to deliver was limited by powerful lobbies concerned at the economic consequences of his intentions. David Cameron, the British prime minister, also had difficulty converting aspirations to policy. On his tour around Whitehall soon after being elected in May 2010 he said he wanted his new coalition administration to be 'the greenest government ever'. Two months later, under pressure to balance the budget, the UK government announced that funding for the Sustainable Development Commission (SDC) would be withdrawn from 2011.[5] This independent body both

---

5 On 22 July 2010, the UK government announced that funding was to be withdrawn from the SDC from 2011.

provided advice and acted as a watchdog to facilitate the transition to a sustainable (greener) society. Despite the green intentions of the politicians, the economic imperatives took precedence.

The aspirations of both the US president and the UK prime minister were soon reined in when the economy appeared to be under threat. Politicians have responsibility across the whole breadth of policy. They need coherent advice from experts, or teams of experts, who can work across both the issues of sustainability and management of the economy.

Rethinking economic globalization

The policies of globalization have brought about a massive shift in the way the world economy operates. Between 1980 and 2007, the ratio of trade in goods and services to global gross domestic product (GDP) rose from about 42 to 62 per cent, while foreign direct investment rose from 6 to 32 per cent. The stock of cross-border international bank loans and other financial instruments rose from about 10 to 48 per cent (Nsouli 2008). It appeared that closer linkages between economies gave greater stability as weakness in one economy could be countered by drawing on financial resources from elsewhere. I put forward a counter-opinion before the financial crisis of 2008 that these interdependencies provide the circumstances for occasional dramatic collapse (McManners 2008: 171–2). When the world economy was booming policy-makers didn't want to look under the bonnet. Following the financial crisis, as the engine has spluttered, people are more willing to acknowledge that globalization is not the panacea it was once thought to be.

The problems with globalization run deeper than the risk of occasional massive instability. An analysis of globalization shows that the economic context in which it is judged is too narrow and incomplete. When society and the environment are included, the policies of economic globalization start to look flawed. For example, the environmental consequences of consumption can be hidden by the open global market. A specific example is European environmental regulations forcing the transition to cleaner, and often more expensive, industrial processes. In an open world market, the dirtiest industries migrate to places such as China, where regulations are less onerous. Europeans can continue to consume and Europe's regional environment is better protected. The consequence is that pollution associated with European consumption is shunted away to China, well away from Europe's residents, out of sight and out of mind.

Across the whole range of the policy agenda, the theory of globalization has had a strong influence. The narrow economic argument in favour of globalization is an agenda with a limited time horizon. The assumption that there will always be more resources available to be sucked out of an open world market is a false assumption. There are limits which will have to be respected eventually (Meadows et al. 1972, 2004). It is important to recognize the need for change as the world navigates a future beyond the era of globalization; the changes will apply to all sectors, including aviation. The events of 2008/09 dented confidence in the model of economic globalization, but most politicians see this as a temporary setback. Rather than rethinking the assumptions behind the model, there are calls for more globalization to recapture the levels of growth of the recent past.

Reconciling economic aspirations and sustainability leads to globalization taking a different form. The priorities for the future are to deliver stable economies that deliver social outcomes for the population and protection for the environment. There can be no dispute that these are desirable aims, but discussion has not yet coalesced towards an agreed alternative policy framework.

There have been attempts to propose alternatives to globalization (Cavanagh and Mander 2004) and books for a committed green audience such as *Green Alternatives to Globalization* (Woodin and Lucas 2004), but these have not garnered widespread support. I proposed an alternative policy framework from a mainstream perspective in the book *Green Outcomes in the Real World* (McManners 2010). The framework includes greater local autonomy and less emphasis on physical trade leveraging know-how across borders to deliver sustainable closed loops of manufacturing, consumption and true recycling. The Sustainable Revolution, which such policy will initiate, will reach into every area of policy, resulting in improvement in human welfare, but it will also be disruptive. One change is that a sustainable world economy is less dependent on the international transport infrastructure.

This insight into a future for the world economy which is less dependent on transportation will not remove people's desire to fly, but it does undermine the argument that the economy requires aviation to be exempt from sound environmental regulations.

Specific policy dependencies

The general point that a sustainable world economy will be less dependent on high-capacity aviation can be tested by considering areas of policy where aviation has a significant role. The specific issues of 'poverty reduction' and 'tourism' are singled out, but first let us consider the role of aviation in facilitating good global governance.

World peace depends on effective dialogue between nations, enabled by technology to provide fast and reliable communications, but this is not sufficient on its own. Communication through technology cannot replicate the rich interaction between leaders and their delegations meeting face to face. Summits between world leaders and the meetings of the G8 and G20 groups of nations, for example, are valuable forums. These meetings could not be staged as often without the rapid transportation that aviation provides.

There are a wide range of conferences and meetings on every possible theme. Some are vital to world security, such as talks on nuclear non-proliferation. Others have lesser importance. I hesitate to name a particular conference as someone is bound to be offended; what is clear is that the meetings and conferences that are most important would happen despite a contraction in capacity that would result from moving quickly to make aviation shoulder the full cost of its environmental impact.

World governance is improved because aviation enables world leaders, and their key advisers, to meet face to face on a regular basis, but this is no reason for special exemption for aviation from sound environmental regulations.

Poverty reduction Aviation's role in poverty reduction is often cited in defence of the existing model of aviation. With air freight inexpensive, there are numerous examples of companies importing produce from poor countries where labour is cheap. At the micro level it is easy to identify particular beneficiaries. This is more often than not the middleman pocketing a profit rather than the primary producer.

UK consumers spend over £1 million each day on fresh produce, including fruit, vegetables and flowers, which is air-freighted from Africa (McManners 2009). Some people argue that such unsustainable food transport arrangements should be banned. Others defend the trade, citing the economic benefits for the farmers, despite the fact that a large proportion comes from farms owned and leased by the importers. This is a trade that would not exist, or which would be confined to a very small premium market, if measures to make aviation sustainable were applied.

Fairtrade products are a special case, providing protection for the small producers to prevent exploitation and ensure they get a fair return for their work. The Fairtrade Foundation defines fair trade as 'better prices, decent working conditions, local sustainability, and fair terms of trade for farmers and workers in the developing world' (Fairtrade 2010). There is much discussion of fair trade and how to deliver the aspirations of the scheme. This is a complex area, not covered in any depth here, except to make the point that it would be inappropriate to base local poverty reduction measures on unsustainable global supply chains.

Helping poor countries through facilitating trade can be a valuable component of poverty reduction, especially if the products are produced under the umbrella of fair trade. However, micro-level improvements cannot be justified if transportation at the macro level is air freight. Of course poorer countries should be helped, but poverty reduction should take place within a sustainable framework. Poverty reduction is no reason for special exemption for aviation from sound environmental regulations.

Tourism Tourism is an important source of income for many countries, and flying is how many tourists arrive. It is argued that flying should be kept affordable to retain tourist income, but this needs closer examination. For a developed country like the UK, visitors come and residents go on holiday. This is a two-way flow of people and cash. In the UK, during the recession, tourism suffered. There were fewer tourists from America, Australia and New Zealand, but there were more people staying closer to home. The mix of tourists would change if flying cost more, but the impact on net cash flow from tourism would be harder to determine. The tourism industry is understandably wary of action to constrain aviation, but the outcome will be different, not necessarily worse, bringing disruption and requiring the industry to be innovative in its response. Besides, tourism is not a sector vital to running society; the potential economic impact on tourism in the developed world is no reason for special exemption for aviation from sound environmental regulations.

For the developing world, international tourism is an opportunity to earn valuable foreign exchange. Not many local people can afford to be international tourists so tourism is expected to deliver positive cash inflow. Less developed countries may have natural wilderness areas which are very important to the global ecosystem, such as the Amazon rainforest or the rainforest of West Africa. There is a strong argument that the country should be able to earn income from conserving these virgin forests through tourism. Tourists arriving by plane have a valuable and positive role in both providing income to the government and giving a financial incentive to conserve the wilderness and its biodiversity. It would be counterproductive if this became a mass low-cost market with low margins, putting considerable pressure on the wilderness with little in return. To fulfil the potential of such tourism it should be aimed at a small premium market, limiting the impact and maximizing the income for the local communities and the host country. Such international tourists are not themselves the poor and vulnerable and can afford to pay a ticket price that fully reflects the environmental impact, so there is no reason for special exemption for their flights from sound environmental regulations. The new economics foundation (nef), a London-based think tank and advocate for real global economic well-being, describes the situation (nef 2008):

> There is a danger throughout the global economy, and not least in tourism, of locking in a self-defeating spiral of over-consumption by those who are already wealthy, justified against achieving marginal increases in wealth amongst the poorest members of society.

The rise of sustainability

The growth of aviation and globalization are interdependent; aviation would not have grown so fast without the policies of globalization; globalization would not have proceeded as far without high-capacity international transportation to move people and goods. The relationship between globalization and aviation is a Faustian pact that locks the world into an unsustainable network of activities. Rather than defend the status quo, discussion has to move forward to the construction of a sustainable world economy and consideration of how aviation meshes with the new sustainable policy framework.

While economic globalization remains the bedrock of world policy, aviation will be protected from the reforms required to significantly reduce its environmental impact. As the policies of sustainability gain ground, this protection will be seen as no longer necessary. Understanding the coming shift in global economic policy is needed to think through how sustainable aviation will evolve. The particular feature of the current economic framework that has had most impact on the aviation industry over recent years is the policy of deregulation, leading to the rise of low-cost carriers. The dynamics of this market segment is where the analysis turns next.

8 | The low-cost revolution

> If it's conventional, it's generally not wisdom. If it's wisdom,
> it's generally not conventional.   Herb Kelleher, chairman,
> Southwest Airlines (Calder 2006)

Low-cost airlines have transformed aviation; pulling many more
destinations into the flight network and offering a wide range
of options to passengers. New customers are drawn into flying
and existing customers are flying more often, facilitated by the
policy of deregulation. This has taken place without regard to
the environmental consequences. As society closes this loophole,
and brings the environment inside policy, the low-cost model will
have to change or be replaced.

The low-cost revolution is regarded widely as a great success,
with the leading low-cost operators consistently profitable in
an industry where profits can be elusive. For government, the
expansion of affordable aviation is seen as vindication of the
policy of deregulation; passengers have more options and pay
less. Cities and regions compete to attract new low-cost routes
to bring people and economic activity to their locality. Aircraft
manufacturers are pleased to be selling more planes. For example,
in Europe, the leading low-cost airlines, Ryanair and easyJet, have
been big purchasers of new aircraft over recent years. Low-cost
aviation appears to be a picture of economic success in which
all stakeholders have done well.

An incisive analysis of the total effects of low-cost aviation
exposes the unwelcome truth that the uncontrolled expansion of
conventional aviation is unsustainable. There has been no mechanism to bring the environment into the calculations by industry
leaders or the decisions made by travelling passengers. Before
deregulation, policy-makers could influence the size and shape

of the industry. As the environmental impact of conventional aviation on the atmosphere became better known, policy-makers could have constrained capacity in advance of the development and deployment of green air vehicles. Instead, they have knowingly and deliberately given up their role in planning capacity and routes, opening the way to massive uncontrolled expansion.

In this chapter the basis of low-cost aviation is examined in order to facilitate an understanding of the rationale for its success and expose its flaws, demonstrating that low-cost aviation is a showcase for how well-intentioned policy can have unintended consequences which undermine the sustainability of society.

The birth of low-cost aviation

Texas in the 1970s was the crucible in which short low-cost flights became popular. The three largest cities in Texas, Dallas, Houston and San Antonio, are all connected by freeways, but the drive between any two cities takes four to five hours. Until Southwest came along, flying was the preserve of the relatively rich. Southwest launched with a flat fare of $20, which it later dropped to $13 for a one-hour flight.

> The Mission of Southwest Airlines is to provide safe and comfortable air transportation ... at prices competitive with automobiles and buses ... (Extract from Southwest Airlines vision statement, 1978)

Southwest's low fares were competitive with those of automobiles and buses, attracting passengers away from ground transport options and encouraging new passengers who might be tempted by a cheap one-hour flight but would baulk at embarking on a four-hour journey.

Herb Kelleher is the father figure of Southwest Airlines and the pioneer of the low-cost model. He used his robust, charismatic leadership to develop Southwest Airlines despite considerable resistance from the established airlines. Leading up to the first flight in 1971, around the triangle of Dallas, Houston and San Antonio, a competitor airline obtained a restraining order. Kelleher persuaded the Texas Supreme Court to throw out the injunction. When the then CEO of Southwest asked Kelleher what to do if the sheriff was still inclined to enforce the order he replied, 'You roll right over the son-of-a-bitch and leave our tire tracks on his uniform.' When flights began the next day the sheriff stayed away (Calder 2006).

The success of Southwest depended on a whole series of innovations, each quite small in effect but, taken together, a winning formula. The general principle was to keep planes flying because that is when they make money; and keep fares low enough to keep people travelling. There was no pre-assigned seating; people got on the plane much more quickly when they were rushing to get the seat they wanted. This reduced gate turnaround time. The company line was that your seat on the plane was reserved – you just didn't know which one. Later the airline would make fast gate turns like racing pit stops, aiming for just ten minutes. The legendary team culture of the airline allowed everybody to join in to make the turnaround, with cabin crew, and even pilots, mucking in as required.

Southwest might have remained a small Texan airline with a unique competitive advantage, but the US regulatory framework was about to change, opening up a whole new market.

In 1978, the Air Deregulation Act was passed by Congress. This opened up the skies of the United States to competition. The old rules that restricted routes, schedules and fixed fares were scrapped. Any airline that could satisfy the Federal Aviation Administration that its operations were safe could fly anywhere in the United States and set the fare at whatever level it chose. This is the foundation on which low-cost airlines were free to expand across America.

Over the three decades since deregulation, Southwest Airlines has grown to become the largest domestic carrier in the United States. It emplaned over 100 million scheduled domestic passengers in 2009. It was also the largest airline in the world (total numbers of passengers emplaned) until the US airlines Northwest and Delta merged in 2009. In Europe, the largest carrier of international passengers is low-cost airline Ryanair, with 65 million passengers carried in 2009 (IATA 2010b).

Expansion into Europe

Ryanair was a small loss-making independent Irish airline when Michael O'Leary was called in by the Ryan family in 1988. Over two decades later, O'Leary is chief executive of Europe's biggest airline. He is a trained accountant with a reputation for tough talking and a keen eye for costs. Ryanair has taken the low-cost model to extremes with the assumption that price overrules any other factor. Not only is there a complete lack of frills but staff can be insistent to the point of being rude if passengers do not comply with the requirements of maximum operational efficiency. Having flown Ryanair into Tampere in Finland, I found the experience more like being treated as cargo than as a passenger, but the flight was much cheaper than those offered by any of the major airlines flying into Helsinki. Passengers get what they expect, a total uncompromising commitment to minimum cost.

Michael O'Leary's role model was Southwest's Herb Kelleher. After being appointed deputy chief executive in 1991, when the airline was close to bankruptcy, O'Leary flew out to Dallas to meet Kelleher and see at first hand the operations of Southwest. Following that visit, the future for Ryanair would be based on flying the maximum number of people at the minimum price. Over the next ten years, the airline grew to become one of the most valuable airlines in the world.

Liberalization was the foundation of growth in Europe following the US lead. The first significant dismantling of controls was the UK–Netherlands bilateral agreement of 1984. The first significant step towards liberalizing the whole of European airspace was a package of measures agreed by the European Council of Transport Ministers in 1987. This explicitly acknowledged that European competition rules applied to air transport (European Commission 1987). This meant that many inter-airline agreements over capacity planning, revenue pooling and pricing were deemed anti-competitive and were progressively abandoned (Doganis 2010). Europe now has a plethora of airlines, including the highly successful low-cost airlines Ryanair and the UK-based easyJet, launched by Stelios Haji-Ioannou in 1995. Recently, eastern Europe has become home to a number of low-cost airlines taking advantage of cheap labour in the regions where their operations are based.

Capacity creating demand

Ryanair's business approach goes beyond adding capacity to match demand. Ryanair builds capacity and then generates demand to fill it. When a new European city enters the Ryanair network it draws in new tourists, providing uplift to the local economy. Ryanair understands the value of the new cheap air route to the local municipality, so negotiates very hard before opening a new route, or deciding to retain an existing one. The airline requires a runway and a terminal building, which might be little more than space in a cargo building. It also expects to pay very little for the use of the facilities. The pressure for the best deal goes farther; Ryanair often seeks, or is offered, 'marketing support' from the local area to bring in paying tourists. It is doing nothing illegal, running a successful business within the letter of the rules.

Creating capacity that stimulates demand, particularly in the creative and hard-nosed manner of Ryanair, is good business for the airline but creating demand also creates environmental stress. Sustainable policy would start with seeking to control demand through reducing the need to fly. Generating demand to fill capacity is the complete reverse of sustainable policy for aviation.

This is a similar dilemma to that faced by power companies. The traditional model is to seek to sell more energy. This is the obvious and simple way to increase revenue and therefore profits, but sustainability requires that energy is used more efficiently and sparingly. The power companies are now entering an era when they must accept that demand reduction is the judicious policy. This has the support of government and engages consumers, who are coming around to the idea that they should buy low-energy appliances and low-energy light bulbs. The energy companies have to be cleverer in findings ways to generate profit from selling less. The low-cost airlines have not yet faced this situation, but it is just a matter of time.

A recent study of the future of aviation in the EU used in-depth interviews with consumers, airlines, airports, air traffic controllers and manufacturers (Bows et al. 2009). A number of scenarios were presented to stakeholder groups and the study concluded that 'even with incremental technical and operational improvements pushed as far as participants believed to be possible, the sector's emissions would only be reduced by 2030 to below 2005 levels if growth in demand for aviation was curtailed. However, the participants had little appetite for explicitly controlling passenger demand.' The stakeholders of the aviation industry can see that the logical consequence of sustainable policy is to constrain demand but are reluctant to accept the consequences. This denial of logic puts the aviation industry behind the sustainability learning curve, and it will suffer as a result.

Road transport is another area where demand management is becoming recognized as an alternative to building yet more roads (Saleh and Sammer 2009). It has been shown that building more roads generates more capacity, but can lead to further gridlock as longer commuting profiles become feasible. Aviation is different because the skies are free. It costs very little investment in infrastructure to open a new route. The cost to society is not taxpayer expenditure on infrastructure, nor good land lost to highways, but a hidden cost in long-term damage to the environment.

The particular insight that Herb Kelleher spotted and others followed, that demand can be created, is a lesson that has to be unlearned. Twenty-first-century aviation innovators have to work out how to profit from flying less.

The low-cost model goes global

There are attempts to take the low-cost model global; if these succeed there will be another huge expansion in global flight capacity. Progress is slow because the parameters are different. A long-haul flight of seven to twenty-four hours is already achieving high utilization of the prime asset, the aircraft. The potential savings from faster turnaround on the ground are less. Also, passengers need to be fed and watered, so a no-frills service is less possible and less acceptable to customers.

Entrepreneurs have been working hard on developing a low-cost long-haul model. An early attempt was Zoom Airlines, a Canadian low-fare scheduled transatlantic airline founded in 2002. It filed for bankruptcy in 2008, blaming its problems on the 'horrendous' price of jet fuel at a time when oil prices reached a record high of $147 a barrel (BBC 2008a). This collapse is an example that will be repeated across the industry when aviation fuel becomes subject to significant taxation; but, for now, with fuel cheap, the low-cost long-haul market has potential. Airlines based in countries with a low cost base are most likely to succeed, such as recent entrant AirAsia X, a long-haul budget airline based in Malaysia which started operations in 2007. AirAsia X is a franchise operation of AirAsia, Asia's largest low-cost airline, and includes Sir Richard Branson of Virgin Group as a shareholder.

Until governments change aviation policy there may be many more budget long-haul operators. The standard low-cost method will be used; generating demand through providing increased capacity and then using marketing to persuade passengers to fill it. The same methods of selecting out-of-the-way (cheap) airfields will be used. Flying from London Heathrow to Sydney Kingsford-Smith will remain relatively expensive. To fly from a remote UK airfield to a small town in outback Australia, to live the life of Crocodile Dundee for a week, could be much cheaper. Although this example assumes a flight from the UK to Australia, it is likely that the operator would be based in the Far East, using local flight crew and maintenance staff, to minimize costs. A budget long-haul operator would have to generate enough new demand to fill the seats and make it pay.

With the right marketing support (marketing in both the normal sense of the word and as a euphemism for subsidy from destinations keen to attract tourists), it is possible that low-cost long haul could take off.

The flaw in the business plan

The premise of low-cost flying is based on two assumptions: first, aviation fuel remains free of tax and therefore continues to be cheap relative to fuel for ground transportation; second, governments don't care about the increasing quantities of aviation fuel burnt by the aviation sector, and this indifference continues. As concerns over climate change grow, these assumptions will no longer be secure. It is right that governments now consider the options and change the parameters on which the low-cost aviation sector depends.

Through the lens of sustainability, the massive expansion in capacity brought about by the low-cost aviation model makes no sense. If policy-makers had understood sustainability, applied the theory and acted upon the insight, they would have introduced regulations to prevent the low-cost airlines from expanding in the way they have.

Enlightened business people, who understand and practise the principles of sustainability, are a new and rare breed, but the numbers are growing. Business people who can see the future would not now invest in a low-cost aviation business plan. It would be clear that it would be only a matter of time before regulations would undermine the profitability of the business and force fundamental change. Unfortunately, such knowledgeable and environmentally aware business people are in short supply.

Graduates coming out of business schools and entering the top consultancies or fast-track corporate programmes have not been well versed in the principles of sustainability. Business schools are very slow to deliver teaching that is appropriate to the environmental challenges of the twenty-first century. Southwest Airlines has been used in business schools for three decades across America and Europe as a textbook example of good business practice. It is a classic example of reading correctly the changing political environment (deregulation) and designing a novel and different business strategy that will carve out a profitable new business. Herb Kelleher of Southwest, Michael O'Leary of Ryanair and Stelios Haji-Ioannou of easyJet are presented as role models for budding entrepreneurs. Stelios Haji-Ioannou is now Sir Stelios, having received a knighthood from Queen Elizabeth II for services to entrepreneurship. These business leaders are exceedingly good businessmen, but from a generation brought up with ideas that will soon be outdated.

All stakeholders are culpable in allowing the low-cost airlines to initiate a massive expansion in the emissions from aviation. Policy-makers and government have been too beguiled by the theory of free markets and deregulation to interfere. The existing airlines have had no choice but to join in with low-price offers and pared-down services; in some cases setting up their own low-cost subsidiary. Passengers enjoy the greater choice and cheaper tickets, and turn a blind eye to the environmental consequences.

The time has come to bring sustainability into aviation and address the flaw at the centre of the low-cost business model. Policy is needed to restrict carbon emissions; sooner or later society will insist on change. All actors in government and the aviation industry should accept this inevitable outcome and plan for a sustainable future.

The death throes of low-cost aviation

The low-cost airlines come from an era that will soon be past. The industry is entering the final stages before the model fails. Low-cost airlines are placing huge orders for aircraft, negotiating ever more obscure destinations, and it is all based on extrapolating historical trends. Massive expansion is predicted and, if the predictions are right, the projected profit figures for the airlines look attractive. This is a good time to maximize the market value of low-cost airlines, but investors should be warned that a tipping point is approaching.

Even before any real action is taken, or major changes in policy enacted, the industry will sense the direction of travel. As soon as it becomes clear that governments will take off the blinkers of unquestioning adherence to the current policy framework, airlines will rush to reconfigure their operations. Plans will be made to axe the least profitable routes. There will be attempts to transfer the ownership of aircraft fleets to leasing companies, even if costs rise in the short term, in order to shift liability off the balance sheet. Shareholders may call for dividends to extract cash out of the companies before the market turns. This would all be part of business responding quickly to new realities. It is in the power of society and political leaders to decide when to call for such change.

The current state of the world aviation industry is dictated by twentieth-century policies beginning with the Chicago Convention and continuing with the policies of deregulation. The low-cost revolution has some way farther to run if the policy framework remains unchanged. The predictions coming out of the industry are for further massive expansion. This will increase overall CO_2 emissions despite steady improvements in the figures for fuel-per-passenger-mile. The time has come to consider a different policy framework to match the new priorities and challenges of the twenty-first century. This will mean breaking the current mould of policy.

9 | Breaking the mould

Business as usual cannot be tolerated ... UN Secretary General
Ban Ki-moon, Cancún, 7 December 2010

Aviation is shaped by world affairs more than any other industry. Flight networks link countries, continents and the peoples of the world. The mould in which the industry is cast includes regulations, public expectations and a highly competitive environment with tight margins. It will be hard for world aviation to break out of the current mould, but aviation has gone through massive upheavals in the past and can do so again.

The particular thrust of policy over recent decades has been deregulation and policies in support of open skies. An unintended consequence has been that the current regulations indirectly forbid the greening of aviation. No government will lead the shift towards a more sustainable model as such action would penalize the airlines with hubs within their jurisdiction. No airline would dare to make their flying operations sustainable because within an open skies policy other airlines would take the business.

Few countries have the scale and influence to attempt a unilateral shift towards sustainable flying operations. The United States could, but the government would face very strong opposition, particularly with regard to taxes on fuel. It would take a huge change in the political climate for the United States to adopt a leadership position. The European Union (EU) also has the scale to lead but would have to work out how to offer protection to airlines based within the EU that would suffer commercial disadvantage.

The recent example of successful mould-breaking in aviation is the low-cost airlines. They have been hugely successful in reconfiguring the commercial dynamics of the industry, expanding capacity, adding new routes and making flying available to many more people. The low-cost airlines might be exemplars of innovative business strategy, but their actions conflict with sustainable policy. It is not these new airlines which are at fault but the regulations that have encouraged their growth.

In this chapter, the current mould of aviation is examined, in the context of introducing taxation on aviation fuel, showing how economics can be used to open the way for green aviation.

The current model of aviation

The current model is firmly established, resistant to change and does not serve society well. For the industry, deregulation means that profits are squeezed and returns are poor. Governments are prevented from raising tax revenue for fear of hitting their own airlines disproportionately hard. For the flying public, there are benefits from a plethora of routes and exceedingly low fares, but everybody involved is neglecting to take account of the environmental consequences.

Aviation has suffered ups and downs, such as the weak economic conditions of the recent recession, difficulties arising from 9/11[1] and unpredictable acts of nature, such as the Icelandic volcanic eruption of 2010. These have had significant impact, but the underlying mould of aviation has held firm and the outcomes have been predictable. A decade ago, Rigas Doganis predicted (2001):

> The airline business will become no different from any other multinational industry. The first decade of the new millennium will finally see the complete transformation of the airline industry from a protected, nationally owned industry into a true multinational business operating freely across frontiers.

Aviation has developed to become the true multinational business predicted by Doganis. The world's biggest airline, taking into account domestic and international operations, was until recently American Airlines but is now United Airlines after its merger with Continental Airlines. The largest operators on international

---

1 9/11 refers to a series of coordinated terrorist attacks upon the United States on 11 September 2001.

routes are:[2] Emirates, Lufthansa, Air France and British Airways, followed by Singapore Airlines, Cathay Pacific Airways and American Airlines (IATA 2010b). The top three airlines for domestic operations are all US airlines, although Chinese domestic airlines are growing fast. Long-haul airlines tend to group in alliances for their potential for increasing profitability (Czipura and Jolly 2007). The industry is dominated by three big alliances: Star Alliance, SkyTeam and Oneworld. These combine marketing and sales effort with operational efficiencies. Some of the savings can be passed on to customers as lower prices or, on routes where competition is erased, used to bolster airline revenue through keeping prices high. These behemoths wield considerable power and influence over the industry, working together with aircraft manufacturers.

Boeing and Airbus dominate the world market for large aircraft. There are long-standing accusations of unfair competition as governments collude to keep these companies strong. Boeing is accused of government support through lucrative defence contracts. Airbus is accused of being in receipt of soft loans from the EU. These are important industries that politicians in the USA and Europe will support insofar as they are able. Each new aircraft model requires enormous investment, with the potential to make or break the company, so great care is taken not to depart too far from proven designs that are accepted by the market. This duopoly has enormous power over the future direction of aviation, dictating the mix of models from which the airlines make their choice.

State airlines used to dominate aviation and still exist in many countries, particularly in South America, Africa and the Middle East. For example, Emirates Airlines is wholly owned by the government of Dubai and is now the world's largest international carrier. State airlines are flying the flag of the nation and often receive government support, as well as benefiting from the home advantage of internal flights, where they may have a monopoly over some routes, and preferential terms at national airports, such as prime landing slots.

---

2 Measured by kilometres flown by scheduled international passengers.

In Europe, open-skies policy has dismantled barriers right across EU airspace with few truly national airlines remaining. The airlines are listed companies owned by international investors. Lufthansa is still recognizably German with 66 per cent German nationality shareholders (Lufthansa 2010). The ownership of International Airlines Group (IAG), formed from the merger of BA with Iberia, the Spanish airline, is more diverse. Open-skies policy is expected to encourage even bigger airline groupings in the future.

Growth in the industry is closely correlated with growth in GDP. As a rule of thumb, based on historic figures, air capacity grows at twice the rate of GDP (CAA 2008). It is assumed that provided GDP keeps growing, so too will aviation. As the countries of the world grow richer, more people are drawn into the group who can afford to fly. Previously poor populous nations like India and China, where most people would not have considered flying as an option in the past, are rapidly catching up with the flying expectations of the developed world.

The deregulation of aviation markets encourages competition between airlines, keeping prices low to the consumer and profits squeezed for the operators. This is, of course, what is expected from a deregulated market, but it is necessary to pause to consider whether there might be factors to consider other than the ticket price charged to passengers.

The current mould of aviation policy will lead to huge expansion over the next two decades. While the current policy framework holds firm, the airlines can invest with confidence in expanding their fleets to match anticipated demand.

The impact of the oil price

When the oil price is low, flying is profitable; when the oil price is high, margins are squeezed and profits suffer. In 1980, fuel costs had risen to between 30 and 33 per cent of airline operating costs and coincided with a period of financial losses (Doganis 2001). Through the 1990s fuel was between 12 and 15 per cent of operating costs. By the end of the first decade of the new millennium fuel costs were again up to around 26 per cent and losses were rising. The spike in the oil price in 2008 that sent prices to over $147 a barrel would have sent the proportion of fuel cost higher still but the price quickly fell back to more affordable levels. In 2011, oil prices resumed their upward trajectory, with some doubt whether a further reprieve is possible as the peak in world oil production approaches and demand grows in developing economies such as China.

The reason that aviation is so sensitive to oil price is that aviation fuel is free of tax. A comparison between US and European car fuel illustrates the point. When a car in Europe is filled with fuel, around 50 per cent of the cost is tax. If oil prices rise by 20 per cent then the price to the car driver rises by around 10 per cent. The oil price shock of 2008 did not hit European consumers as hard as the United States, where taxes are much lower.

If the world had the courage to put a significant tax on aviation fuel, aviation would be much less sensitive to the price of oil. Heavy taxation on aviation fuel would bring more stability; it would also mean substantially higher fares. Such action would lead to a more stable, more expensive and smaller industry; in summary a more sustainable industry. The logic for a tax on aviation fuel is strong but the reality of implementation is complex. It is necessary to show that taking this courageous decision, although bringing short-term restrictions, will set the circumstances for the transformation to a model of aviation that is appropriate for the twenty-first century.

Predictions of the future

Forward predictions of the market are important for the aviation industry. When a new aircraft model comes into production the production line will run for many years. Boeing's 747 production line opened at the Everett site in Washington State in 1967. The first 747 flew in 1969. The production line is still running over four decades and 1,400 planes later (Boeing 2010). The majority of these aircraft are still flying; some with up to forty years' service (Norris 2010).

It is expected that many of the planes now coming off production lines will still be in the air in the middle of this century. The design parameters given to the aeronautical engineers and designers are based on the current view of future trends. Often these are extrapolations of past trends. While there is certainty that the current mould for the industry will be retained, the predictions are fairly accurate. But when the mould is broken, which will have to be the case eventually, all predictions will have to be abandoned.

The new parameters will be determined by what the politicians decide to do, which will be very hard to second-guess. Politicians should signal their intentions early and make firm commitments. Aviation will then have the parameters needed to plan for the future. Until politicians act, the industry is working on figures extrapolated from twentieth-century aviation trends. Instead, aviation needs a new direction for the twenty-first century.

Airlines and manufacturers need to second-guess the regulatory framework that will apply in the future. Their first reaction is to lobby government for action that will be favourable to their current business. A more nuanced approach is to consider what governments will be forced to do in the end through pressure to act on climate change. Lobbying to continue exemption from the full environmental cost will get harder. My suggestion to the industry is to make the first move and lobby in favour of taxation on aviation fuel. This would lead much more quickly to a firm basis on which to plan the future. In the short term this is less favourable to the industry as it will force contraction, but certainty provides a sound basis for the businesses that will thrive in the twenty-first century.

There is a win-win situation that presents itself, if world governments want to take it. The immediate gain for government is increased tax revenue. To make the situation palatable to the aviation industry will require regulatory change. Instead of focusing on open skies, governments should focus on sustainable aviation. This will achieve two outcomes. First, freeze out the countries and airlines that choose to stay outside sustainable aviation. Secondly, regulate the market so that it is easier for the airlines that tackle the green challenge to make profits to invest in making the transition. I believe that governments and industry working together could construct a tax regime and market mechanisms that would generate income for government and protect the profitability of those airlines that lead the transformation. The environmental reasons for such a course of action are sound, but of course the resistance will come from business and the public objecting to more expensive flights. In a democracy the public will have to be persuaded that this is sound policy before politicians will act.

There is no guarantee that the transition to sustainable aviation will commence soon. The prime axis of the debate is between those who champion globalization (and the role of aviation in connecting economies) and environmentalists. This book hopes to play a part in bridging the gulf, but the differences are too great to lead quickly to a meeting of minds between these two camps.

It is possible that major change is still twenty years away. The predictions of 'climate change' and 'the end of oil' may take time to become reality. The issues may connect, as it now seems certain that as the world warms the Arctic Ocean will become ice free each summer. Oil companies are already planning how to exploit the opportunity. There may be substantial new oilfields inside the Arctic Circle that can delay peak oil. Oil prices may rise but remain at affordable levels. It is also likely that the worst predictions of climate change, such as significant sea level rise, will not impact most of world society over the next two decades. There will be excuses available over the short term to avoid taking substantive action.

With regard to aviation, from the point when it is decided that real action is required to the replacement of the world fleet of conventional aircraft will take thirty years or more. Delay the decision point when this process starts by twenty years and that is fifty years of delay. Allowing half a century more of conventional mass aviation is hardly sensible, but that would be the consequence of failing to break the current mould.

Using economics to redesign aviation

Economics is a powerful intellectual discipline but useful only if it works in support of society. This is evidently true, but economists have made their models so complex that there is a danger they lose sight of this underlying truth.

Policy-makers often work on the assumption that the best economic outcome is the best solution. In a complex world it is hard to take into account every factor, so this simplification makes decision-making easier. The core assumption is that economic progress and wealth correlate with human welfare. For very poor societies there is some truth behind the assumption, but it is now known that for rich societies increasing wealth does not lead to greater happiness (Layard 2005). For poor societies, economic progress has to be linked to welfare gains for the whole population; improvements that feed through to increasing wealth for a few people in the ruling elite improve the headline figures but do not give the true picture.

It must be recognized that economic analysis is only one component of any decision and this is at the core of operating a sustainable society. This applies also to the quest for sustainable aviation.

The key statistic in the airline industry is cost-per-passenger-mile. Purchase decisions and fleet management choices hinge on this figure. It can be assumed that green 'aircraft' will have a higher cost-per-passenger-mile at the outset. Over time, economies of scale will drive down costs and competition between manufacturers will drive down prices. Economics is playing its role in mediating between the players in the industry, rewarding innovation, selecting the winning technologies and supporting the strongest companies.

However, society has other priorities. When the cost-per-passenger-mile of green air vehicles is known this insight can be used in setting the floor for taxation on aviation fuel. Society can then control the introduction of green aviation and accept on behalf of passengers that flying will cost more. Economics is used correctly as the mechanism to implement the policy of reduction in the environmental impact of aviation.

The cost-conscious mass market will shift to green air vehicles. Fast flying will be confined to senior leaders in government and industry, key experts and the very rich. These people, or the organizations that employ them, will pay a high price. The benefits will flow back into society through taxation. For political acceptability, and to satisfy the concept of fairness, it will be necessary to channel tax income into increased investment in improved ground transportation that is available to all, such as improved rail networks.

There is an obvious attraction to attempting to search for a mechanism that will facilitate the transition to greener aviation without it costing more. This requires bringing complexity into the economic model and obscuring the figures. The simple economic truth is that in a sustainable policy framework conventional flying will cost more to provide economic justification to develop and deploy a new fleet of green 'aircraft' (discussed in Chapter 11). This is the logical outcome of making the changes; but in a society that puts the emphasis on narrowly defined economic metrics, policy-makers will resist and passengers will complain.

Breaking the mould

Breaking the current mould of aviation will require bold action from politicians and willingness to abandon long-standing entrenched policies.

There is one pivotal action that will break the current mould. This requires removing the implicit guarantee, provided by the Chicago Convention, that aviation fuel remains free of tax. This situation is skewing business decisions away from sensible sustainable policy, undermining preparations for the future beyond oil and spiking the business case for the development of alternative fuels and aircraft.

Until society sees climate change as an emergency, there is little appetite for breaking the current mould and initiating a period of disruptive change. Meanwhile there are other actions that can be taken, many of which are sensible improvements, but these are too little, too late.

10 | Too little, too late

Aviation has progressed with military requirements as a prime driver of the underlying technology, within a policy framework that is now over sixty-five years old. The only areas where the reduction of environmental impacts has been given a high priority are in the vicinity of airports. So, for example, noise from aircraft (a very obvious problem) has forced manufacturers to make their aircraft quieter. Exhaust pollutants are also a local problem with regard to air quality; therefore the International Civil Aviation Organization (ICAO) has regulations to limit pollutants from aircraft engine exhausts, but the limits apply only during the Landing Take-Off (LTO) cycle. It is only recently that CO_2 emissions have been discussed, and there are no regulations to limit them.

The development path of aviation has been shielded from effective environmental controls; this has taken the industry into a policy cul-de-sac with no easy way out except to reverse and find another way. The reason that policy-makers conspire with the industry to motor ahead without selecting reverse gear is strong resistance from the general public to constraints on their options to fly. It is therefore necessary to examine carefully all possible actions with the potential to reduce the environmental impact of aviation without a major shift in direction. These marginal changes to aviation can deliver improvements and deserve analysis because of the difficulty of reining back the industry to set it on a sustainable path.

This chapter examines current efforts to bring emissions from aviation under control, including the potential of carbon trading and the aspirations of the aviation industry to improve its environmental credentials. The overall conclusion is that the delay in starting the transition means that current plans are too little and too late.

Carbon trading

The concept behind using international market mechanisms to limit carbon dioxide emissions is that, as the world shares one atmosphere, the impact of emission reductions is the same regardless of where they are made. However, as carbon markets are established, the difficulties and limitations are becoming evident. Although carbon markets facilitate reductions in the short term, and achieve lower costs, the medium- and long-term implications are worrying.

All carbon markets need a cap that is enforceable and screwed down more tightly over time until emissions have dropped below a safe limit. The Kyoto Protocol is the first stage on the route towards a global cap on CO_2 emissions; it specifically excludes aviation, agreeing instead to 'pursue limitation or reduction of emissions of greenhouse gases ... from aviation ... working through the International Civil Aviation Organization' (UNFCCC 1998). Even if aviation were to be included in a successor agreement, it is doubtful that the world community would be able to agree and then enforce a binding global cap on CO_2 emissions. The danger of reliance on a weak global market is that despite the fact that over the short term there is a shift to cleaner fuels and therefore fewer emissions, over the long term the market ingrains reliance on fossil fuel into the world economy, smoothing the transition to dirty fuels as reserves of the cleaner fuels decline. Markets for trading CO_2 have potential to help society to make the transition to other energy sources, but their role is useful at the national or regional level, where it is possible to enforce an effective cap (McManners 2010: 63–6).

In the absence of an effective open global carbon market, aviation would need a closed market in which allowances or permits were traded within the aviation sector. Initiating the market would require distributing permits among the airlines, which would be fraught with difficulty as airlines and countries fight to secure allocations. Free allocation of permits based on past emissions is one method, but this would hand windfall profits to the least efficient airlines and be unfair to new airlines in the developing world without a past history of high emissions. The more effective method of allocating permits would be through a global auction, with decisions required on which organization would run the auction and how the proceeds would be collected and distributed.

The establishment of a closed carbon market for aviation, working to a tight cap on emissions, could, in theory, constrain emissions from the aviation industry until dramatically more efficient air vehicles could be designed. From a sustainable policy perspective this would seem to be an appropriate outcome, but the industry would struggle with uncertain costs on which to base investment decisions. The cost of permits could rise dramatically but then fall back again as capacity was removed and older aircraft taken out of service. This uncertainty regarding the price of permits in the future would be a major hindrance. To be effective, a closed carbon market would need a floor price, or an equivalent measure such as a tax on aviation fuel, to give a firm foundation for future investment.

The ICAO has rejected a closed carbon market for international aviation, arguing that the high relative costs of aviation technology and the lack of substitute energy sources mean that it is not cost effective compared with reductions in other sectors (ICAO 2008). The ICAO prefers to encourage aviation to join existing emissions trading schemes, the largest of which is the EU Emissions Trading Scheme (EU ETS).

In July 2008, the European Parliament voted to include all flights in the EU ETS from 2012, including flights from outside Europe. 'For the period from 1 January 2012 to 31 December 2012, the total quantity of allowances to be allocated to aircraft operators shall be equivalent to 97 per cent of the historical annual emissions' (over the period 2004–06), decreasing to 95 per cent in subsequent years (EU 2008).

In a briefing paper for the European Parliament, the effect on aviation of its inclusion in the EU ETS was examined, including a comparison of a closed and an open trading system (Anderson et al. 2006). The paper concludes that 'a stand-alone system is likely to be far more stringent, as mitigation costs are generally higher in aviation than in other sectors, diminishing the likely attractiveness of the approach. From an economic point of view, an open trading system with a clearinghouse mechanism would be the favourable option as it uses the mechanism of the trading market in its most efficient way.' The consequence of aviation fully integrated into the EU ETS is that the most economic choice for airlines will be to buy carbon credits rather than invest in emissions reduction, thus delaying, rather than initiating, change.

Carbon markets are likely to have a useful role at the national or regional level, where it is possible to enforce an effective cap, but aviation is an international business with very long time horizons and high levels of investment which needs firm economic parameters. A closed carbon market within aviation has potential, but linking aviation into regional carbon markets would appear to be flawed, allowing the purchase of credits at artificially low prices. Carbon markets could have a role in aviation but only if such distortions are removed by the introduction of additional measures, such as a tax on aviation fuel, to provide a firm economic basis for long-term investment.

In defence of cheap flights and continued growth

There is an argument, used by the aviation industry, that climate impacts can be addressed without constraining capacity or pushing ticket prices higher. This is an enticing argument which attracts support. The elements of such a utopian solution include improved aircraft efficiency and better air traffic control to reduce delays and make routes more direct. These are measures that are needed in any case and will deliver savings but, in an industry that is growing fast, they will not be enough to bring overall emissions under control. The action proposed by the aviation industry is:

Airlines, airports, air navigation service providers, and manufacturers share a common vision for aviation and climate change. Their commitment includes capping net CO_2 emissions from 2020 with carbon-neutral growth and aiming toward a 50 per cent reduction in net CO_2 emissions by 2050 compared with 2005. (IATA 2010c)

The aviation industry is coming under pressure to bring carbon emissions under control; developing targets that pre-empt action by politicians is a good tactic that may delay the introduction of regulations. The IATA proposals need further examination as they are not as ambitious as they seem. First, these are non-binding aspirations that can be altered easily. Secondly, using long-term targets deflects attention away from the proposed near-term actions. Thirdly, the 50 per cent reduction in *net* CO_2 emissions by 2050 compared with 2005 is not what it seems. Gross CO_2 emissions from aviation will continue to rise substantially; the industry's aspirations are based on an unrealistic massive shift to biofuels, arguing that, as these carbon dioxide emissions are not from fossil fuels, they can be taken out of the reckoning.

Biofuels will be an important energy source for aviation (discussed in detail below) but it is highly unlikely that sustainable biofuels will be available in the quantities required to match demand across the economy; claiming that a large proportion could be used in aviation is disingenuous. The UK Committee on Climate Change (UKCCC) is more realistic in its assessment, stating that 'it is not prudent to assume that biofuels in 2050 could account for more than 10 per cent of global aviation fuel. It is likely that use of aviation biofuels will be both technically feasible and economically viable. However, there will be other sectors which will compete with aviation for scarce biomass feedstock' (UKCCC 2009).

There are a number of possible actions that can be taken to reduce the CO_2 emissions from aviation, as measured by CO_2 per passenger kilometre or CO_2 per tonne of air cargo. The key question is whether these can deliver sufficient overall reduction. If not, the course of action to reduce the environmental impact will have to constrain capacity. For an industry with projected profits based on continued growth, industry insiders will work very hard to ensure that capacity restriction is not adopted as the sustainable solution – even though it is the obvious way forward in the near term.

More efficient aircraft

Efficiency comes from three main sources: better aerodynamics, lighter weight, and more efficient engines. Recent developments in aerodynamics include the winglets that are becoming universal at the end of the main wing on most aircraft. These improve air flow and reduce drag. Weight reduction in commercial aircraft has been led by the 787 Dreamliner design team through making extensive use of composite materials in the construction. Improvements in aero engines include the geared turbo fan. Jet engines have fans that suck air into the combustion chamber, where it is compressed, mixed with fuel and ignited. It then goes through a turbine, generating thrust. This is less efficient than it could be because the fan is connected to the engine and turns at the same speed as the turbine. Fans work best at low speed, while turbines work best at high speed. Pratt & Whitney have solved the problem with a gearbox that lets the fan and turbine spin independently, creating a quieter, more powerful and more efficient engine. It is claimed that it will burn 16 per cent less fuel than the best conventional jet engines when it comes into service (Pratt & Whitney 2010).

The Airbus A380 and the Boeing 787 are the newest generation of production aircraft with many of these features. Fuel economy figures are better than three litres per passenger per 100 kilometres when flying at full capacity, with claims that the 787 is 20 per cent more efficient than the aircraft it will replace. The fuel efficiency of the world fleet will improve as these models progressively replace older aircraft.

The IATA has set a target to improve aircraft fuel efficiency by 1.5 per cent per annum up to 2020. This figure is on a par with the average improvement that has been achieved over the last decade as older, less efficient aircraft are retired. So the target is a reflection of the continuation of business-as-usual. Delivering the reduction requires that airlines continue with plans to purchase large numbers of new aircraft. There is a direct dependency between the expansion of fleets (and increased total CO_2 emissions) and the promised per-passenger efficiency improvement. The information presented by IATA is accurate but also misleading.

Better air traffic control

While I was writing the draft of this chapter on a flight from Stockholm to Heathrow, my flight was delayed and circled to the east of London for thirty minutes waiting for a slot to land. Circling to no purpose, watching the jet exhausts, brought my words to life. Busy airports often stack planes, which burn fuel going nowhere. Improving flight management systems could reduce or eliminate this wasteful activity.

In other instances, aircraft are forced to deviate from the shortest direct route to comply with air routing corridors and rules. It is also common that aircraft gain altitude or descend in steps according to instructions from air traffic controllers. It would save fuel to allow aircraft to climb at the optimum rate and then carry out a glide descent that uses the least possible fuel, determined by the parameters found through analysis of operational data. The aircraft autopilot could be programmed with the most efficient flight profile. For this to work, air traffic control systems would have to be able to manage the increased complexity of less standard routing.

The prime task of air traffic control is, of course, safety. The old manual systems needed very clear route and altitude separation. Advanced automation, fed by data from on-board GPS systems, could support much more sophisticated air traffic management while retaining sufficient safety margins. Efficient flying requires flying direct without deviation and then descending on the perfect glide path to land without delay. It is estimated that 1.4–6.0 per cent fuel can be saved through efficient cruise trajectories (Clarke 2010).

Capacity planning is another constraint. Runways can accept

flights only at a set interval, typically two minutes. Each plane needs time to safely leave the runway before the next plane touches down. An airport working at full capacity will be forced to stack planes if there is any disruption. This is the argument behind calls for a third runway at Heathrow, the world's busiest international airport. Proponents claim that the increased capacity will reduce delays, while opponents worry that this will generate yet more traffic. Better traffic management will improve overall efficiency but needs to be part of much greater change.

Use of biofuel in aviation

On 24 February 2008, a Virgin Atlantic 747 jumbo jet flew between London's Heathrow and Amsterdam using fuel derived from a mixture of Brazilian babassu nuts and coconuts in one of its four engines. Sir Richard Branson claimed, 'This pioneering flight will enable those of us who are serious about reducing our carbon emissions to go on developing the fuels of the future.' Representatives of Friends of the Earth described the flight as a 'gimmick' and 'high-altitude greenwash' (BBC 2008b).

Despite doubts about the true sustainability of biofuels in aviation, the momentum to increase their use is growing. In June 2011, a Boeing 747-8 landed at the Paris air show after crossing the Atlantic with all four engines running on 15 per cent biofuel mixed with traditional jet fuel. In the same month, the European Commission, Airbus, leading European airlines and European biofuel producers launched the 'Biofuel Flightpath' with the aim 'to ensure the commercialisation of sustainably produced paraffinic biofuels in the aviation sector by reaching a 2 million tons consumption by 2020. For this, it is necessary to ... support the construction of industrial "first of a kind" advanced biofuel production plants.' (Maniatis et al. 2011).

In the search for alternatives to fossil fuels, biofuel seems like an attractive option, allowing replacement of fossil fuel with biofuel, requiring minimal change to the transport infrastructure. The basic principle is that biofuel can be produced from a wide range of biomass ranging from farm crops and forestry waste to human sewage and industrial organic waste. Such biofuels are sustainable because the feedstock comes from the natural carbon cycle, using the process of photosynthesis to fix the energy from sunlight with CO_2 out of the atmosphere. When the biofuel is burnt the CO_2 is returned to the atmosphere. Provided the cycle repeats to fix more CO_2, this is a sustainable closed-loop process that could go on indefinitely.

When considering biofuels, we need to be aware of one particular pitfall. Processing crops into a usable biofuel requires energy, which must be subtracted from the calorific value of the biofuel. Incentives to grow biofuel crops can lead to attempts to rig the markets and create perverse outcomes, for example producing biofuel that requires a similar amount of energy input to process. This processing energy can come from a low-tax fossil fuel, such as coal or agricultural diesel. The resulting biofuel can be used in road transportation, sidestepping the heavy taxation applied to fossil fuels in this sector. The net result is profit for the producer, but tax revenue loss for the government, with agricultural land taken out of food production – and at the end, the same amount of fossil fuel has been burnt. Care is needed that aviation does not fall into the same trap as taxes are introduced on aviation fuel.

First-generation biofuels are made from agricultural crops such as ethanol, derived from maize, or biodiesel from palm oil. In a hungry world, switching a large proportion of agricultural capacity from food to fuel leads to rising global food prices and greater pressure on natural resources, such as clearing virgin forest to make way for palm oil plantations. It is increasingly understood that first-generation biofuels are limited in their ability to achieve targets for oil substitution (Sims and Taylor 2008) and are not the sustainable solution to curing the world's addiction to fossil fuel.

Second-generation biofuels are derived from farm and forestry waste, such as non-edible parts of food crops and tree clippings, as well as non-food crops grown on marginal land not suitable for agriculture, such as switchgrass. Steam heating is often used to break down the tough stems with research being undertaken into enzymes that can make the process more efficient to increase the net energy output. These second-generation biofuels will be a very useful component of the energy mix for the future, especially when integrated into small-scale facilities close to the source of the waste without recourse to fossil fuel in the production process. It could be possible, for example, to decarbonize farming by generating all the energy needed to run the farm and its machinery through energy from farm waste. However, second-generation biofuel will have many demands on it and will not be able to replace current levels of fossil fuel consumption across society.

The third generation of biofuels show more promise. The principle is to use closed tanks containing algae, or some other organic or chemical process, to convert the energy from sunlight into a liquid hydrocarbon fuel. The beauty of these fuels is that the production could be located in desert regions using land that has no other purpose. The problem is the extensive facilities required, using considerable resources in construction, putting a question mark against the sustainability of the process and ensuring that third-generation biofuels will be expensive. Early stage research indicates that another process may become viable using halophytes – plants that flourish in hot, desert conditions with the advantage that they can thrive on salt water instead of fresh water.

The demand for biofuels worldwide will be huge; biofuel is discussed as the solution to low-carbon ground transportation, for heating buildings and in power generation. These supplies cannot be counted twice or thrice over. The world will have to live within the capacity available. The situation could improve if advanced third-generation biofuels fulfil their promise, but it would not be sensible to factor this into policy until the technology is proven, and it seems certain that such fuel will be an order of magnitude more expensive to produce than conventional oil.

Supplies of sustainable and affordable biofuel will be limited. In a world struggling to reduce reliance on fossil fuels, earmarking a large proportion of this capacity for aviation makes no sense. Aviation will use biofuel in future-generation green aircraft but only as one component of much greater change. In the near term it would be better, in an industry where safety is paramount, to keep with the proven aviation fuels such as Avgas and jet fuel, leaving biofuel for use in ground transportation.

Short-term action

Real action to address the environmental impact of aviation must look at what can be done within a short time frame. Policymakers can be held to account for their actions while there is still time to make adjustments.

Researchers at the Smith School of Enterprise and the Environment (SSEE), Oxford, have examined the future of aviation in their *Future of Mobility Road Map* (Inderwildi et al. 2010). As a theoretical exercise, they considered the possible CO_2 emission reductions if immediate progress was made in a range of improvements currently under discussion (noting that this would be impossible). The study looked at achievable engine efficiency improvements, the introduction of biofuel, structural improvements (for better aerodynamics and weight reduction) and fuel savings from operational efficiencies. Over the period it was assumed that all aircraft sales would be of the new, more efficient type. The theoretical effect on total CO_2 emissions from aviation was estimated over the period 2009–14. Despite the improved efficiencies across the fleet (6 per cent) this was more than counteracted by the increase in total fleet size of an additional 1,155 aircraft. The overall result of the exercise was a 1 per cent increase in CO_2 emitted from aviation by 2014.

The solution has to look beyond current plans to something more ambitious and ensure that passengers are also part of any solution. The UK Civil Aviation Authority carried out an assessment of trends in the growth of UK air passenger demand (CAA 2008). They found little evidence that passengers were responding to information about the environmental effects by forgoing air travel in order to reduce their carbon footprint:

There has been much recent publicity in the UK media concerning the environmental effects of air travel. If this reflected a change in public attitudes and behaviour then it would be expected that passengers would choose to forgo air travel in order to reduce their carbon footprint – either through using alternative modes or destinations, or by not travelling at all. However, little evidence supports this.

The CAA concluded that, 'traffic growth in the near future is more likely to be affected by changes in the cost of aviation rather than attitudes of passengers to the environmental effects of flying'.

The CAA assessment and the SSEE analysis show that passengers and the aviation industry, if left to get on with it, will not make reductions in the carbon emissions from aviation. The deduction that can be drawn from both studies is that the current discussion about change in aviation is not radical enough.

There are no realistic and substantive plans to reduce the environmental impact of world aviation, with the projected expansion outstripping the savings from improved efficiency. The aviation industry expects to continue with little deviation from business-as-usual up to 2020. Beyond 2020, the industry is presenting a solution based on a massive and unrealistic shift to biofuel. This is too little, too late. The world is on track, without substantial change of policy, towards a climate crisis. The aviation industry is locked in denial and on track to collapse under regulatory self-destruction through holding to the policy of tax-free fuel for far too long.

The worst effects of climate change can still be avoided. For much of the current aviation industry, it is too late; denial has been going on too long. Society should call a halt and set aviation on the path to a sustainable future, removing protection to allow the circumstances for a transformation to greener aviation.

THREE | **The future of aviation**

11 | Green air vehicles

Low-emission aircraft will look radically different to the current generation of conventional planes. Modern computers and advanced wind tunnels allow weird new shapes to be tested; so any shape is in the frame for the pioneering task of the next generation of highly efficient aircraft.

Current aeronautical design builds on a wealth of data gathered over decades of flying, from numerous air crash investigations and the careful examination of airframes at the end of their working life. Designs are refined and weaknesses addressed, moving ever closer to the 'perfect' design. Incremental improvements in design are expected to deliver yet further efficiencies, but engineers are coming towards the limit of what is feasible in further refinement of conventional aircraft.

In this chapter, it is shown that it is possible to build and deploy green air vehicles, drawing inspiration from nature and using existing capabilities, leading to an aviation industry with a significantly lower environmental impact.

Barriers to progress

The main barrier to significant progress in reducing the environmental impact of planes is that factors other than fuel efficiency have driven design. With fuel so cheap, the designers have been able to concentrate on speed, range and capacity. A study in 2005 compared the last piston-engine aircraft of the mid-fifties to a typical modern turbojet aircraft. The large piston airliners used as the baseline for the study were the Lockheed Super Constellation L-1049, the Lockheed Starliner L-1649A and the Douglas DC-7C. These workhorses of 1950s civil aviation had energy intensity per available seat-kilometre of 0.9–1.7 MJ/skm,[1] considerably more efficient than 1.9–2.9 MJ/skm for the Boeing B707 series, which were the first jetliners produced in large numbers. Recent models of turbojet aircraft, such as the Airbus A340-300, the Boeing 777-200 and the smaller Boeing 737 operate in the range 0.9–1.3 MJ/skm, reclaiming the fuel efficiency of the 1950s propeller-driven airliners. The study concluded that fuel efficiency per seat-kilometre had not improved (Peeters et al. 2005). Aircraft have got faster, fly higher and farther, but burn amounts of fuel similar to those consumed half a century before.

The challenge is not just aircraft design – the whole infrastructure of aviation is stuck in a rut. The case of the Airbus A380 shows that technological advances are delivering improvements; the A380 is reported to be 12 per cent more fuel efficient than the Boeing 747-400. This could have been greater if optimum fuel efficiency had been a higher priority in the design parameters. A further 10 per cent improvement in fuel efficiency may have been possible if the wing aspect ratio had been designed for maximum aerodynamic efficiency. However, airport handling constraints defined by the ICAO for the largest Code F aircraft limit the A380 to a wingspan of 80m.

The current generation of aircraft is going through one last refinement of the conventional design, replacing aluminium alloys with carbon fibre composites. This construction method will save weight and therefore reduce fuel burn, but even this small enhancement (small compared with the scale of the coming changes) is proving to be hard to implement. Both Boeing and Airbus have delayed new models while they get to grips with the new methods. In the conservative world of the aircraft industry, development moves slowly with every stage double- and triple-checked. This care and caution is essential to safe flying but is not conducive to making the leap forward to low-emission air vehicles.

---

1 Energy intensity per available seat-kilometre is expressed as a range to show the impact of different cabin configurations.

A vision of green air vehicles

The task of delivering green aviation would be a wonderful challenge for the engineers if they were given the freedom to explore a wide range of solutions. The general parameters of possible solutions can be identified to replace the current design of a cylindrical fuselage, to carry people and freight, fitted with wings to provide lift. These new designs are one aerodynamic body shape that both carries the cargo and provides lift without a clear distinction between wings and fuselage. The capability might be improved by including spaces filled with helium; not an airship but using lighter-than-air buoyancy to contribute to overall performance. It is likely to be large and a fairly flat shape with a huge area of solar cells to power electric motors turning highly efficient propellers. The solar power will enable cruising in the reliable sunshine found above cloud height. It will have other power sources for take-off, emergencies and when unavoidably heading into a head wind. In a design that uses a lifting gas, helium is the safe choice, but the design could also include large sections of compressed hydrogen or a hydrocarbon gas to be used for fuel cells or gas turbines, to provide additional power during the take-off phase until the aircraft climbs above the clouds.

There will be trade-offs to be made between minimizing fuel consumption and overall performance parameters. The target of being able to cruise on solar power alone may be possible only in ideal conditions. What is achievable will depend on a mixture of factors too complex to predict until the engineers have been given the freedom to experiment. Some factors will be technical, such as advances in the efficiency of solar cells; other factors will be operational, such as the minimum speed that the airlines and passengers will accept. There may be different models and different operating modes depending on the route and the markets being served.

I put forward a design brief for such an aircraft in 2008, being careful not to be too prescriptive to give engineers and designers an open brief (McManners 2008: 91). If the world regarded climate change as a severe crisis on a par with the world wars of the twentieth century, this design would have had the backing of a war cabinet and the prototype could be flying today.

In 2010, I discussed the idea of a green aircraft with an eminent engineering professor. The discussion moved quickly to the conclusion that it could not be done. Probing further, I discovered that this was not a stubborn rejection on the grounds that the engineering could not deliver; because there is little doubt that such a craft can be built. The rejection of the concept was based on assumptions outside of the design brief.

The key assumption that was holding back further consideration was that green aircraft should cost the same or less to operate than conventional aircraft. The assumption was that pure economic considerations trump other factors.

Finding a solution to moving people and cargo by air using a craft with low environmental impact is not simple and the result may be different to the vision presented here. When a feasible design emerges, attention will shift to how the customer experience of such a craft will be different and how operations would be managed. For example, a low-emission craft will certainly be slower than conventional jet aircraft. If solar power is a prime energy source once at cruising altitude, schedules will have to take into account daylight. Route planning will also have to take into account prevailing winds as these will influence range and speed.

These are all interesting issues to ask the aviation industry to solve. There are already a number of developments in aviation technology that could be employed, but until the economic framework of aviation changes there is no incentive to make progress towards the vision of green aviation.

Learning from nature

To reduce the environmental impact of aviation, it seems appropriate to turn to nature for inspiration. This follows in the footsteps of Leonardo da Vinci, who used observation of the anatomy and flight of birds to help to sketch ideas of how a flying machine might work, and the Wright brothers, who derived inspiration from observations of pigeons in flight (Howard 1998).

The early aviators had to advance beyond observation to understanding the dynamics of flight to be able to build machines that harnessed the principles. With knowledge of the science of aerodynamics, humans are now capable of designing a huge range of flying machines.

Modern aircraft design has moved beyond the lessons of nature to deliver supersonic and hypersonic aircraft. There are few lessons to draw from nature in such extreme flying. Nature has been left behind – and ignored. The environmental impact of flying is not a concern to most people and, until recently, reducing it has not been specified in the design brief given to aeronautical engineers. Fuel economy is a feature because it is an important metric in the economic operation of aircraft fleets, and no more important than that.

In navigating a sustainable future for aviation, biomimicry is becoming important again. Biomimicry is learning lessons from nature by careful observation and then re-creating technical solutions using the principles uncovered. The winglets that sprout from the wings of new aircraft, and are retro-fitted to older aircraft, are an example. These smooth the flow of air around the wingtips, reducing drag and improving fuel efficiency. Engineers working on the A380 claim to have drawn inspiration from the steppe eagle, a bird of prey native to Europe and Central Asia (Airbus 2010). The eagle's wings are perfectly shaped to maximize lift. It can manipulate the feathers at its wingtips, curling them to create a 'winglet', a natural adaptation that aids highly efficient flight.

Biomimicry will help the designers in the search for an aircraft that can soar above the clouds with the same grace as a steppe eagle, using thermals and atmospheric conditions to its advantage, with little more environmental impact than the birds. Instead of sticking to fixed routes and schedules and throttling up the jet engines to make headway despite the weather, flight planning will become much more complex, taking into account forecasts of wind speed and direction. Flying in tune with nature requires flexibility to work with the opportunities that weather systems provide and patience to travel at the most efficient speed for the conditions. Air traffic controllers and pilots will have to find ways to balance a complex system with few fixed parameters. Achieving this and retaining safe management of the airspace will require a new generation of air traffic control systems.

When green air vehicles come to market, airline executives will have a marketing opportunity to feature flying with the birds. The image of flying that is often sold today is of service during the flight and the attraction of exotic destinations. This is because advertising executives have to find images that draw customers' attention away from images that suggest the process of flying, such as engine exhausts and vapour trails. Flying like a bird is a very attractive image, but when used to sell seats on a conventional aircraft will invite accusations of greenwash (the making of environmental claims that do not stand up to analysis). Before green-spin marketing can be activated, without generating a backlash, the engineers have to be given an appropriate brief to deliver the technology that truly allows planes to fly with as little environmental impact as the birds. The leading companies in this new age of aviation will not need to rely on huge advertising budgets; the news gatherers and documentary film-makers will tell the story for free.

As Charles Lindbergh noted before he died, the construction of an aeroplane is simple when compared with the anatomy of a bird. The complexity gap is going to close as computer-controlled green aircraft take to the skies flying like the birds, dependent on complicated cooperation between meteorologists, pilots and ground crew informed by satellite data in real time.

Learning from the military

The military have large budgets to drive forward development. There may be little apparent overlap between military needs and green aviation but where there are technologies, paid for by defence, that could be useful in the design of low-carbon planes, ways should be found to leverage the technology beyond the defence sector.

Flight control systems from military aircraft will have applications in green air vehicles. The first aeroplanes were built with a body with large wings towards the middle and small tail wings towards the rear. This is a naturally stable configuration. Without moving the controls such aircraft tend to fly straight and level. Modern fast jet fighters have a reverse configuration with small wings towards the front and bigger wings towards the rear. This configuration is inherently unstable but allows for incredibly fast manoeuvring. Human pilots are not able to fly such aircraft without computers operating the controls to retain stability. The same may apply to some of the advanced highly aerodynamic designs that green aviation will use, with the task of piloting delegated to computers.

Advanced low-drag aerodynamics is another area where defence has the leading technology. The US government decided during the Cold War that it wanted a stealth bomber that could deliver bombs while remaining invisible to radar. This top-secret programme was pursued with little regard to cost, taking further the concept of a jet-powered Flying Wing heavy bomber aircraft developed by Northrop for the United States Air Force shortly after the Second World War. The Northrop YB-49 first flew in 1947, but the prototypes were destroyed, keeping the technology out of the public domain. Further development was kept secret, leading to the B-2 Spirit (stealth bomber) which had its first public flight in 1989, but it is thought to have been flying for many years before this. The attraction for the military is that the ultra-sleek shape has a very low radar signature, making it virtually invisible to anti-aircraft defences.

The shape that makes the stealth bomber invisible to radar also has high aerodynamic efficiency, giving the B-2 long range. This shape is the preferred shape for the next generation of fast civilian aircraft because of the fuel efficiency and therefore lower carbon footprint.

In the Cold War, this was a valuable capability and funds were found. It is estimated that the cost of each B-2 stealth bomber was over $2 billion (General Accounting Office 1997). If it were possible to pursue the concept of green aviation, at any cost, it would be interesting to see what designs would emerge. I am confident that green aircraft can be designed and built. I am also sure that they would cost less than $2 billion apiece! However, as with all novel designs, it is to be expected that the costs will be more than for conventional aeroplanes until the technology embeds into the industry. The military approach to finding a technical solution to a vital operational need – at whatever cost – could be applied to designing and building green air vehicles, if governments allocate the task a high enough priority. There may not be the bottomless budget of a vital defence requirement but increased costs do not need to be a barrier; governments can tax aviation fuel and/or carbon emissions to ensure that green air vehicles have a commercial advantage when the total-cost-of-ownership is calculated.

Propulsion technology

The big leap forward in the middle of the last century was the jet engine, designed in the search for ever more speed for military fighter aircraft. Dr Hans von Ohain and Sir Frank Whittle are both recognized as inventors of the jet engine, working separately in the closing years of WW2. The German turbojet engine was first to fly in 1939, with the first flight by Frank Whittle's jet in 1941.

The attraction of the jet engine is that it can operate at higher speeds than propeller aircraft, which are limited in the speed they can achieve because of shock-wave formation when airflow approaches sonic speeds. The Russian Tupolev Tu-114, built from 1955, still holds the record for the fastest propeller-driven aircraft at 540 mph (Mach 0.7). The plane had counter-rotating propellers on the front of each engine which helped it to cope with the high speed (compared with other propeller aircraft). This was a very reliable, safe aircraft, but it was soon replaced by the Ilyushin Il-62 jet airliner, which began production in 1963. It is interesting that the maximum speed of the Ilyushin Il-62, at 560 mph, is not much greater than that of the more fuel-efficient plane it replaced; so, in this case, designers accepted less fuel efficiency for a quite small increase in speed.

In the West, the most successful early jet airliner was the Boeing 707, with over one thousand built from 1958 to 1979. The Ilyushin Il-62 jet became the standard Soviet long-range airliner, with over 300 manufactured from 1963 until 1995, with many still flying today. The high operating costs (due to high fuel burn) are leading to more of these aircraft retiring and being replaced by newer models, but, while aviation fuel is cheap and the residual value of the planes is very low, it can make commercial sense to continue operating such aircraft.

The jet engine now dominates aviation, with modern jet engines reported to be about 70 per cent more fuel efficient than the first jet engines. This statistic is often quoted to show the excellent progress that has been made in jet engine design, neatly sidestepping the fact that only the most modern aircraft exceed the fuel efficiency of 1950s propeller-driven passenger aircraft.

There are further efficiency improvements in the pipeline for jet engines. Current-generation high-bypass jet engines have a giant opening at the front feeding air into a giant fan, turned by the jet, which delivers thrust by moving a large mass of air relatively slowly around the outside of the combustion chamber, helping to smother the noise of the jet exhaust gases. A further development is to make this fan into an open rotor using two rings of counter-rotating blades, a bit like returning to propellers and with some similarities to the Tupolev Tu-114. In some respects aviation is backing off from fifty years of development to regain the fuel efficiency of the 1950s to be able to progress along a different path.

Another development is the orbiting combustion nozzle jet engine, which the designer, Dr Lior of R-Jet Engineering, claims offers up to 25 per cent more fuel efficiency compared with conventional jets of similar power (Economist 2010b). The engine is designed such that the air passes through the combustion chamber as a spinning vortex, mixing the fuel well for complete combustion and eliminating the need for two sets of static blades (the diffuser and stator) used in conventional jet engines. This new design is being developed for static small-scale highly efficient energy generation plants. When the technology is proven, it could be deployed as the power source to turn open rotors to propel the next generation of green air vehicles.

When efficiency replaces speed as the prime design parameter, new aircraft with propellers or open rotor jet engines will come into service. The technical innovation to be exploited would have been available three or four decades back if policy were not locked into a framework of cheap fuel.

Next-generation aviation fuel

Where speed is essential, propulsion technology will continue to use high-density liquid fuels with innovation focusing on the source of the fuel. Third-generation biofuel has potential (biofuel is discussed on pages 107–10). For example, the US Navy has tested algae-based jet fuel in a Super Hornet jet fighter (Kay 2010).

The search for a sustainable liquid fuel does not need to be confined to biofuel. The world's deserts are a huge potential resource of renewable energy from the sunshine that radiates on to barren land and is wasted. Whatever is done to capture this energy will not conflict with other land-use priorities. The challenge is designing and implementing a cost-effective method to convert the sunshine into a liquid fuel. Conventional oil is one example, where sunshine was captured by vegetation millions of years ago and, over geological time, processed into crude oil. Nature has done the work for us; now we need to use our technology to capture today's sunshine. The resulting fuel could be hydrogen, a biofuel or a hydrocarbon fuel designed by scientists. At this stage it is important not to stifle innovation by being too specific; this is why I use the term 'liquid sunshine' to avoid second-guessing the engineers and scientists (McManners 2008). Provided engineers can devise a process to make liquid sunshine that is practical and affordable, then the world will have the means to harvest the renewable energy that shines each day on the world's deserts.

Liquid sunshine is a concept that needs an engineering solution. The production facilities will have to use limited resources in their construction, or have a very long lifespan, to make the concept sustainable. The solution is likely to be clever but simple, using bioengineering based on algae or another organism genetically engineered for the purpose, or techniques and methods not yet devised. There are plenty of deserts in North Africa, in Australia and even in the home of conventional oil, the Middle East. For now, there is no incentive to develop such a solution. Liquid sunshine will need considerable investment and the fuel will be significantly more expensive than products derived from oil. Oil production costs are so low that liquid sunshine could not be competitive within the current economic context.

The affordability parameters that will be applied to liquid sunshine when the world breaks its addiction to fossil fuel will be different. Setting a high price penalty on fossil carbon emissions and heavy taxes on fossil fuels will place liquid sunshine in a different competition. Instead of competing with coal or oil, the competition will be against fuels derived from other sustainable sources, including, in the far future, a new generation of clean nuclear power using fusion technology. The current and next-generation reactors using nuclear fission produce radioactive waste, a legacy that will remain the responsibility of future generations long after the energy has been consumed and the reactors closed down. The long-term benefit of current nuclear technology is as a stepping stone to harnessing nuclear fusion, the process that takes place inside the sun. This is technically demanding and still many decades from fulfilment but could deliver clean power in abundant quantities, but this too will not be cheap. Liquid sunshine could therefore remain commercially viable into the long future, but progress towards that future is delayed until society severs reliance on cheap fossil fuel.

Greener propulsion will attract considerable research and investment when efficiency replaces power and speed as the prime design parameter. Significant taxation on aviation fuel will change the design parameters and increase the pace of innovation. This should give policy-makers the confidence to face down resistance and push through policy for sustainable aviation, knowing that beyond the short-term pain the future is bright.

Hybrid air vehicles

There is a new class of air vehicle that will have an important role in sustainable aviation, having attributes of both airships and aircraft, using a combination of lighter-than-air gas buoyancy and aerodynamic lift. These hybrid air vehicles are larger and more rotund than an equivalent aircraft but flatter and more aerodynamic than an airship with a similar load capacity.

A study for the US Congressional Budget Office (CBO), 'Options for Strategic Military Transportation Systems' (CBO 2005), provides a useful insight. It looked at a comparison between purchasing a fleet of fifteen Hybrid Ultra Large Aircraft (HULA) for $11 billion compared with twenty-one C-17 aircraft for about the same budget. The heavy-lift airship under consideration is the proposed Walrus HULA designed to lift 500–1,000 tons up to 12,000 miles non-stop and then land without a runway. The report assessed that the HULA fleet could deliver three times as much cargo per day as the C-17s. The report does not recommend purchasing the HULA because of the risk and uncertainty of buying an unproven design and the concern that if the C-17 production line were closed down it would be expensive and cumbersome to restart it. A strategic defence concern was over the low altitude and slow speed:

> Overflight rights might be more difficult to obtain for airships because their passage would be much more apparent than that of a conventional aircraft. Consequently, nations willing to quietly allow high altitude overflights might be more reluctant to permit low, slow overflights by airships. (Ibid.: 24)

It is interesting to note that the report acknowledges that technical challenges inherent in the Walrus's design can be overcome. This is a military report in which environmental advantages do not feature. The report shows that HULA is a viable alternative for air freight transportation, being technically feasible and affordable. The sensitivity that the military have to a slow low-flying air vehicle should not prevent its use for civilian freight. However, if the military do not fund its development the investment will have to come from elsewhere.

The development work by the Defense Advanced Research Projects Agency (DARPA) on the cancelled Walrus project has not been lost. Aeros, which claims to be 'the world's leading lighter-than-air, FAA-certified aircraft manufacturing company' (Aeros 2010), intends to take the technology forward, having carried out work for DARPA on its Buoyancy Assisted Lift Air Vehicle (BAAV) programme. The company, based in California, has plans on the drawing board for its Aeroscraft to be able to carry a pay load of 60 tons.

In the UK, a commercial company, Hybrid Air Vehicles, has a flying prototype and is hoping to raise funds to bring its Sky-cat range of air vehicles into production. They claim that the Skycat will use less than a third of the fuel consumed by conventional aircraft. They further claim that 'CO_2 output can be reduced to zero' (Hybrid Air Vehicles 2010) if hydrogen is used as the fuel source.[2] Converting conventional aircraft to run on hydrogen is difficult because of the large space taken up by storage tanks, but hydrogen storage in airships is straightforward.

There are number of other small airship companies around the world, but overall the sector has more ideas than investment capital. Given the US military research it is possible to be confident that the technology will deliver on its promise. The lack of funding is because conventional aviation is protected and very good value for money if the environmental consequences are ignored. Airships will take off when conventional aviation is made to pay for its environmental impact. When this happens, the venture capitalists will be competing with each other to put their money into hybrid air vehicles.

Blended-wing aircraft

Boeing is working on civilian blended-wing aircraft. Two X-48B technology demonstration aircraft were built by Cranfield Aerospace in the United Kingdom to Boeing's specifications. These subscale prototypes have a wingspan of just over twenty feet

---

2 Whether this is zero CO_2 depends on the source of the hydrogen.

powered by three small turbojet engines providing a maximum combined thrust of about 160 lbs. The X-48B has an estimated top airspeed of 118 knots (139 mph) and a maximum altitude of about 10,000 feet and flight duration of about forty minutes (NASA 2009).

There is speculation that there may be plans for a Boeing 797 blended-wing-design aircraft at Boeing's Phantom Works research facility in Long Beach, California. Such a plane could have a lift-to-drag ratio a spectacular 50 per cent better than the new Airbus A380. The blended-wing shape has better structural integrity and stiffness so can be 25 per cent lighter for the same strength. Overall it could be 33 per cent more efficient than the Airbus A380. The design is thought to have similar dimensions to the A380 to be able to use the same airport facilities and may carry up to a thousand passengers (Aviationexplorer 2010). Boeing is secretive about its future plans so it is not known how much truth there is in this speculation.

The newest Boeing aircraft in production is the 787 Dreamliner. It is the world's first mostly composite commercial aeroplane and, according to Boeing, it will use 20 per cent less fuel per passenger than similarly sized aeroplanes. Its launch in 2007 was the most successful commercial aeroplane launch in history, with orders taken for 677, worth more than $110 billion (Boeing 2007). The Dreamliner's maiden flight took place on 15 December 2009 and it is expected to enter service in 2011. This plane is at the beginning of its payback period.

Boeing will be using commercial judgement in planning its future models, but it will be very wary of taking any action that may undermine sales of the Dreamliner before banking the $110 billion from advance orders. The board of Boeing will keep the 797 – if such a design exists – under wraps until the Dreamliner production line has been running for many years.

The transformation

There are enough ideas and prototypes that could be the basis of green aviation to give confidence that the technology will work. Military research and military aircraft have paved the way. The engineers know hybrid large aircraft are feasible and blended-wing aircraft like the stealth bomber can be made to fly. For green aviation, the missing stage is an explicit design brief to deliver low-carbon air vehicles because there has been no commercial reason to do so. With aviation fuel tax free and limited application of carbon taxes the investment case for green aviation does not add up.

When the first-generation jet aircraft entered the aviation industry in the 1960s and early 1970s the technology was disruptive in terms of its performance and capabilities, allowing planes to fly high and fast. The technology of green air vehicles is also a disruptive technology, allowing aircraft to fly with dramatically lower environmental impact. It took fifteen years (1956–71) for jet aircraft to account for 80 per cent of the total aircraft fleet in the United States (Kar et al. 2010: 21–2). It will also take time to develop and deploy the new generation of air vehicles. The engineers have to be given the task, without further delay, to start the transformation that will take aviation into its third golden age.

12 | The third golden age

I confess that in 1901, I said to my brother Orville that man would not fly for fifty years ... Ever since, I have distrusted myself and avoided all predictions. Wilbur Wright, in a speech to the Aero Club of France, 5 November 1908

Green aviation seems to be impossibly difficult to deliver, but not because of technical problems. The knowledge required – in aerodynamics, propulsion technology and advanced materials – is available. The know-how that is lacking is that of how to shape the political and economic context.

In this chapter, ways to break the stalemate that grips aviation are investigated, ways that can lead to dramatic changes in the industry as a new set of constraints, and some old parameters with different priorities, provide the circumstances to launch the third golden age of aviation.

Breaking the stalemate

Operating the industry according to out-of-date economic parameters is preventing progress. It is not just the problem of tax-free aviation fuel but also the dead weight of sunk costs. The investment in the current aircraft fleet and ground infrastructure is significant, representing a large proportion of the value of the balance sheets of the airlines, airports and associated businesses. In a recent analysis of CO_2 emissions reduction measures by the Massachusetts Institute of Technology (MIT), it was found that 'Technology measures in the form of next generation aircraft have the highest CO_2 reduction potential, but only in the long term due to slow fleet turnover' (Kar et al. 2010). The short-term economic perspective leads to the industry focusing on generating returns from the existing assets. The airlines need to keep generating income from their aircraft by keeping them flying. Aircraft manufacturers want to continue to sell current models and get back their huge investment in research and development; this applies particularly to new models such as the Airbus A380 and Boeing 787, which are at the beginning of their production lives.

A useful alternative perspective is to consider designing a world transport system from scratch, with all the technology and knowledge available. This includes all that has been discovered about aerodynamics and propulsion systems for aviation, as well as the possibilities of advanced trains and ships. In this huge store of knowledge there is also information on the impact of emissions on the atmosphere and recent insights into the risks of meddling with the climate. Taking all this knowledge and insight together, the world transport system would be unlike the current system.

Making the case for green aviation

Making the case for the greening of aviation is particularly difficult because the beneficiaries are hard to identify. The direct impact of aviation on people is confined to the vicinity of airports. To build a new airport, or to expand an existing one, requires dialogue with a range of stakeholders. It is likely that residents' objections will focus on noise; therefore those who live directly under the flight path will have to be compensated. Local government can be persuaded by promises of jobs and inward investment that benefits the region. The discussions can be long and drawn out but eventually a balance is found between the parties and the airport is built (or extended). If opposition is severe, the airport may be built somewhere else where the local community values the benefits more and is willing to tolerate the impacts.

The drive for green aviation is a different class of problem. The negative effects that need to be eliminated are the engine exhaust gases, in particular the greenhouse gas, carbon dioxide, but also pollutants such as nitrous oxide which have greater impact at high altitude than the same emissions at ground level. The potential damage is long-term and afflicts the whole world community.

These problems of aviation do not respond to local, or even

national, dialogue. The exhaust gases are soon blown out of the airspace of one country and diluted in the shared global atmosphere. This leads to a particularly difficult negotiation. Instead of competing parties seeking to find compromise there is only one party that will benefit and that is the global biosphere. All other parties – government, the aviation industry and passengers – have to accept constraints, so the people making the case for the biosphere face formidable opposition.

Despite the description of an impossible negotiation between a silent party represented by weak advocates (environmentalists speaking for the integrity of the biosphere) and powerful vested interests represented by professional communicators, it is possible to face down opposition and push for change. It is beyond dispute that the biosphere is important and retaining its integrity is vital, so the crux of the discussion is whether exhaust gases are a threat to the biosphere. The dissenting voices are now very few, which opens the way for substantive discussion of policy options.

A bushfire throughout aviation

The birth of green aviation within a relatively short time frame requires mimicking nature and allowing a bushfire to blow through the industry, destroying the old and making way for the new. Bushfires are an intrinsic part of the ecosystem in places such as Australia, where the natural systems have evolved with fire and numerous species depend on fire to regenerate. The immediate aftermath is blackened trees apparently devoid of life. It is not long before the green shoots of renewal appear. When I was a young boy living in Australia, my family went on a picnic in the bush outside Sydney. I had a great time running around exploring and poking at things I shouldn't. When we packed up to go home I was in trouble. Looking at the abundant vegetation you would never have thought that at the picnic site we had chosen there had been a bushfire the year before. The charred remnants were still in evidence beneath the new growth, enough to make an inquisitive boy black from head to toe.

Changing the economic parameters of aviation will send a

bushfire through the industry. In the short term there will be a contraction in capacity and older, less efficient planes will be sent for scrap, despite having many flying hours left in their airframes. The ground infrastructure, built around the standard parameters of the current fleet, will have to be redesigned when the needs of the next generation of air vehicles become clear. Out of the ashes the phoenix of green aviation will be able to rise.

When entering the maelstrom of a massive step-change, planning and forecasting become difficult; detailed predictions are necessarily inaccurate, but the general direction can be ascertained. The predictions that follow spring from the impossible starting point of a blank sheet of paper. This is impossible because people are anchored in the here and now, but it is insightful, because a better future is easier to envisage when historic baggage is removed. The only assumption used is that society has become serious about protecting the integrity of the environment so that there is a willingness to apply all our technical capabilities to the challenge.

The phoenix rises

Sustainable aviation will conform to a new set of constraints and some old parameters with different priorities. As fuel becomes much more expensive, fuel efficiency will be much more important; and because speed increases fuel burn, speed will therefore become more expensive; so green flying will therefore become rather slower flying, except for those passengers willing to pay a heavy premium. The trade-off in the new era of sustainable aviation, for cost-conscious passengers, will be trading time for cheaper flights.

Oil price A record peak oil price was set at $147 a barrel in mid-2008 but this had dropped back to $30 a barrel by December 2008 as the financial crisis slowed demand. Weakness in the global economy continued through 2009 and 2010, suppressing the price, but in 2011 the price of crude oil resumed an upward path, reaching $120 a barrel in April 2011. It can be expected that

133

oil prices will continue to climb to new records as increasing demand from fast-growing emerging economies such as China exceeds available capacity. This will affect aviation, an industry in which fuel costs are a major factor. If aviation fuel remains free of tax, this pressure alone would lead to marginal change. A doubling or tripling of the price of oil will not seem disastrous; people in the industry might feel that they can relax and allow a smooth evolution to marginally more efficient flying. My assessment is that relying solely on the oil price to drive change would lead to the slow strangulation of green initiatives, making space for deniers to resist reform.

Climate change While the world does not care enough about the risks of climate change, aviation is allowed to be a special case, but when the world decides that climate change is a clear and present danger to the stability of world society, aviation will be in the firing line. Taxing aviation fuel in conjunction with rising oil prices will produce a powerful compound effect. The phoenix of green aviation will start to ruffle its feathers in anticipation.

Technology The current economic context is keeping the technology of green aviation grounded. When airlines know that they will be paying a significant tax on aviation fuel, the engineers and designers will gain their freedom. The phoenix will get ready to fly.

Business Astute business leaders will have foreseen what is coming and made preparations to exploit the opportunities. The new aviation entrepreneurs will lead and public anger should land on the politicians, who did so little for so long, and on those in the aviation industry who resisted most strongly. Clever politicians will dodge the public ire by hiding behind the collective responsibility of international action to counter climate change. The business leaders who failed to see the coming changes will not be so lucky and may be out of a job. The phoenix will be cleared for take-off.

Sustainable aviation takes off

Sustainable aviation is a win-win outcome; people will continue to be able to fly and the environment gets protection. The government can look forward to collecting more tax, which it could use to invest in improved ground transportation infrastructure, or pocket for other purposes. When it becomes clear that sustainable aviation is coming, passengers will book their next foreign holiday quickly before the next ratchet up of tax on aviation. For the industry, there will be a short-term surge in cash flow as people take cheap flights while they are still available. This will be a welcome short respite to help the industry prepare for the restructuring to come.

The direct specific changes required within the industry will come about when politicians set the context and force the industry to react. A positive attribute of capitalism is that it can support such massive change. The industry can throw up its arms and claim that the politicians have made their business unaffordable. This will justify the airlines going into pre-packaged insolvency procedures. The old corporation can leaves its debts and liabilities behind and a new entity can rise up with those assets that fit the future plans. The banks that own the debt and the shareholders that didn't see it coming will carry the losses.

When it is understood that society will insist on sustainable aviation, fund managers and bankers will start to get twitchy. Fund managers required to hold a broad range of shares may be reluctant to sell their holdings in airline shares while there remains a potential upside. Hedge funds have more freedom; when they start dumping and shorting airline shares it will be the start of the endgame. Until that happens, investors can still make money from aviation shares. It may be some time before society takes climate change seriously, so investors may miss out in the short term by avoiding airline shares. However, there should be no sympathy for the banks and investors who stick with the old investment strategies too long and are caught in the lurch when sentiment turns.

The world could make substantive progress towards sustainable aviation over the next decade. It would take up to five years to design and deliver the new air vehicles that are needed. Another five years would be needed to build enough to form a decent-sized fleet. The top-level structure of the market is likely to be much the same as it is now, with three prime segments: first class, business class and economy. I predict that two new subcategories will emerge: 'premium green' and 'value green'.

First class

The rich like to travel in style and are prepared to pay for the privilege. For people who could be described as the idle rich, having both time and money, the new passenger segment 'premium green' will be established (see below). For other first-class travellers, such as world leaders in business or politics, time is critical. Flying has to be both fast and comfortable to enable them to arrive fresh and ready to work. For this group, first-class travel in conventional aircraft will still be required for some time.

The sustainable international flying network for time-poor passengers will use the newer conventional aircraft now coming into service. Where there is high demand for premium flying on routes such as London to Hong Kong or London to New York, the Airbus A380 will operate. On routes with less demand, or where greater frequency is demanded, the Boeing 787 Dreamliner will be used.

The flying experience in first class will be largely unchanged, the only difference being much more expensive ticket prices. This segment is not particularly price sensitive so the drop-off in the number of first-class passengers may not be great.

For many other routes, between less popular destinations, fast, efficient small jets will be in demand. Research carried out by NASA's General Aviation Propulsion (GAP) programme offers an example of affordable efficient engines for the commercial market (NASA 2000). The Eclipse 500, a six-passenger jet, uses EJ22 turbofans, which are commercial derivatives of the GAP FJX-2 turbofan. The manufacturer claims that the Eclipse 500 is 'the most fuel-efficient twin-engine jet available today' (Eclipse Aerospace 2010).

For the super-rich and world power brokers, the private corporate jet is the favoured mode of transport. As the impact of conventional aviation on the atmosphere becomes a greater concern, shareholders and public opinion will be highly critical of the indulgence of individual corporate fast jets. In November 2008, the heads of the three big Detroit auto companies travelled to Washington in separate private jets to make the case to Congress for $25 billion in loans to keep their companies afloat. Politicians were outraged at the extravagance; Congressman Gary Ackerman complained:[1] 'Couldn't you all have downgraded to first class or jet-pooled or something to get here?'

As jet-pooling and jet-sharing services expand, corporations will be able to specify the corporations with which they are willing to share flights. Advanced IT systems will arrange the schedule to minimize the number of flights. There could be many informal and useful encounters with suppliers, partners and customers through pooling executive jet capacity. The car industry CEOs travelling to Washington from Detroit could have shared one private jet and had a useful discussion on the way to prepare for the grilling from members of Congress. The demands of greener aviation will lead to new ways for senior executives to network.

The days of the mega-rich showing off with conspicuous consumption, flying in large private jets complete with gymnasium and Jacuzzi, are numbered. Such bling is becoming unfashionable as 'eco chic' gains ground as the new fashion trend (Black 2008). Even those who can afford such extravagance will choose instead to demonstrate their wealth through flying premium green.

Premium green Premium green is a passenger segment that does not yet exist. It requires a large, relatively slow air vehicle, using some of the innovative design parameters discussed in Chapter 11, including a combination of lighter-than-air buoyancy and

---

1 'Stabilizing the Financial Condition of the American Automobile Industry', US Congress Financial Services Committee Hearing, 19 November 2008.

aerodynamic lift. The propulsion system will include power generated from solar PV cells fitted to the entire upper surface of the air vehicle, requiring that schedules will be daylight flights taking off in the morning and landing in late afternoon. Routes will be selected based on weather and wind patterns, taking advantage of trade winds at low altitude and the jet streams at high altitude.

No pictures of the prototypes under development are reproduced here lest it imply a specific recommendation. Engineering innovation has been held back by a weak economic case. As this is corrected by ensuring that the economics work in favour of green air vehicles, other constraints should not be introduced. Engineers need the freedom to explore and propose novel solutions. Airlines and policy-makers will have to work out the total infrastructure requirement. Different operational schedules will need to be adopted to suit the air vehicle capabilities. Customer expectations will have to be managed and marketing techniques developed to sell premium green.

In such a large air vehicle, premium green passengers will be able to have small cabins and a whole range of high-quality entertainment, exercise options and fine dining. The craft could settle for the night in beautiful remote locations with the minimum of ground infrastructure, to rise into the dawn the next day for the next leg of the flight.

Leisurely grand touring in modern cruise ships of the sky could become common in the travel plans and social diaries of the wealthy, travelling with an entourage of A-list passengers. This would be conspicuous indulgence but not conspicuous consumption, the new eco chic on display.

Premium green will expand beyond its initial market as entrepreneurs think ahead to ways to arrange conferences or senior management away-days that combine meetings with travel. Currently, senior international executives spend a lot of time going through the aggravation of international flights, checking in for an evening flight to go to a hotel in another city for the next day's meeting. Administrators will find ways to organize schedules to exploit premium green, such as arranging meetings on board, with the outcome that senior executives will achieve a better quality of life. Exactly how this would work will become clear only when premium green is established and the market evolves to exploit the possibilities.

Premium green needs an engineering solution. Appropriate air vehicles will emerge when the world takes action that strengthens the economic case to design and build them.

Business class

Business travel is a cost in time and money; managers try to minimize both. This segment will respond very quickly to price signals. Expensive tickets will focus the minds of budget holders, with all options under consideration.

Videoconferencing facilities are already good but could get massively better. The technology is available to build 3D interactive environments in which participants seem to be in the same room; but this is expensive. The costs of flying are used in developing the business case for advanced virtual conferencing, limiting the budget available. If flying were more expensive, the development of virtual reality meeting facilities would be speeded up. This would combine with the increasing power of computers so that the high-end technology used, for example, in flight simulators for pilots could migrate to specially fitted-out corporate conference rooms. The future capabilities will amaze and astonish. Such meetings will save on flight costs and time. This last point could be the most attractive to business. Regardless of concerns over climate change, this will be an advance in the effectiveness of executives.

There will also be business demand for much better ground transportation. Trains are needed that travel efficiently from city centre to city centre with a good working environment. This would include broadband communications and facilities to ensure that time on the train is as effectively used as time spent in the office. This will come without the irritation of shuttling to the airport at each end of the journey. It would be feasible to deliver a train network that replaced short-haul flights with a moderate extension to overall door-to-door travel time. This increased journey time will be balanced against the increased effectiveness in the way the time is used.

For long-haul business flights, the same modern conventional aircraft that carry time-poor first-class passengers would also carry business class (with less luxury and less personal space). These flights, using conventional aircraft, may be first-class and business-class only as all tickets will be expensive, so there may be no place for a no-frills service. The concept of an economy class might survive, in the sense that some seats could be relatively less expensive, but these will not be the low-price tickets available now.

Economy

Economy flying is highly price sensitive. The contraction that would follow large increases in ticket prices may drive economy passengers off conventional aircraft altogether. In the longer term this would be an improvement, supporting the development of the new segment, value green (see below). In the early stages of the transition to sustainable aviation, economy passengers will be priced out of the market. People will have to re-engage with local and regional holiday destinations. Where international air travel is used for foreign holidays, it will be for the occasional main holiday. The flying weekend break from London to southern Europe or from New York to the Caribbean will be too expensive for most people, but even with this group the evolving requirements of eco chic may make such behaviour unfashionable.

The change to sustainable aviation leads to a different mix of affordable leisure travel and holiday options. These need not be worse, but there will be disappointment that long-haul holiday destinations will become less affordable, so a new segment will open up to fill the vacuum.

Value green The same generic class of air vehicles that will deliver premium green will also be used for value green. These large, relatively slow air vehicles will have plenty of space in which to move around. Entertainment could include bars, restaurants, cinema, disco, promenade deck and shops. In value green everything will have a price and private reserved space would be limited to just one reclining seat. Observation windows may be limited but these will be supplemented by screens showing the view outside with a number of camera angles to choose from. Those on a tight budget might sit reading or watching TV, nibbling snacks they carried on board. Others might be in the mood to party throughout the trip, making the journey an integral part of the holiday. Instead of enduring being crammed into a conventional plane and losing that time out of the holiday, value green will take more time, but that time could be spent getting the holiday off to a relaxing start.

A day's journey will depend on the maximum distance that the engineers can squeeze out of the design brief. Assuming that at least 1,000 miles is feasible, this would be enough to go from London to the Mediterranean, or New York to Florida. A long journey to the other side of the world would require a series of hops over a number of days. Range would not be a standard figure, with some routes having favourable wind patterns that could be exploited, and the solar gain around the Equator could deliver more renewable power than at northern latitudes.

Long-haul journeys would become, by necessity, grand tours. Rather than flying on sequential days the journey could include a couple of days at each stopover. This could be a very enjoyable way to holiday for those people with more time than money. Students might use their long vacation to explore the world, flying value green.

Value green could be a revolution in exposing ordinary people to the beauty of the natural world. Instead of flying at high altitude from one concrete terminal to another, the journey could take in stops at out-of-the-way places. Low-cost flying today disconnects people from the natural world, leading to indifference to the environmental impact. Value green could allow people to enjoy and savour nature. Slow travel, with breaks to explore interesting places, could be a much better experience than the current standard package holiday.

The initial losers, when world leaders trigger the transition to sustainable aviation, will be the less well off who can no longer afford to fly. This is political dynamite. Value green, if brought in quickly, could dampen smouldering discontent before it explodes into a backlash against the brave politicians who trigger the green aviation revolution.

Air cargo

The transition to a sustainable air cargo market will be simpler and quicker than changing passenger expectations. Users of air-cargo services are well versed in making commercial decisions, so they will recalculate the numbers and alter supply chains accordingly. Some cargo will shift to rail and sea; in other cases, a decision will be taken about manufacturing location to deliber-ately shorten supply chains. Changing transport costs, by making flying significantly more expensive, will change the commercial dynamics of global sourcing. This should be recognized as an effective lever to a more sustainable world economy and should not promote resistance to increasing the costs of air cargo.

A scenario of the future

The sustainability of the Travel & Tourism industry and that of the environment are mutually dependent. Using its role as an international conduit for peace and prosperity, the industry is actively engaged in the protection of fragile ecosystems and indigenous communities ... Travel & Tourism's far-reaching benefits position it as a leading player in a strong, united, global effort at combating climate change.

This is the view expressed in a joint communiqué from the World Travel & Tourism Council and the UN World Tourism Organization (WTTC 2009a). It is just 'greenwash' while the international travel industry is based on conventional aviation. Rather than asking the travel industry to rewrite their words, I would like the industry to live up to the aspirations expressed. The task is challenging, and will meet with resistance from vested interests, but the prize is worth the effort. The WTTC is correct in their analysis (WTTC 2009b):

> Travel & Tourism companies that adapt and integrate sustainable business practices into their product and service offer will be best placed for medium and long-term success. Recent data from consumer survey groups and Travel & Tourism organisations demonstrate that consumers are increasingly willing to trade up for sustainability, with the result that operators are now allowing 'conscientious consumption' to drive development into the future.

The travel industry has little choice but to endorse the targets set by their colleagues in the aviation sector (ibid.: 21), but travel industry executives need to understand that the degree of change will be much greater than people in the aviation industry are expecting.

Every prediction made in this chapter comes from looking beyond a step-change. When an industry is shaken up to this extent the outcome is uncertain. I am confident that putting down firm foundations, by insisting that aviation must be sustainable, leads to better long-term solutions. The future portrayed could be disputed, but it is my hope that it will be a vibrant future and better than I forecast.

13 | Unleash the entrepreneurs

The vision of aviation outlined in the previous chapters requires action to make it reality. Fortunately there are inventors and entrepreneurs waiting for circumstances to change to exploit the opportunities. This includes research centres run by the existing aircraft manufacturers, which could respond if society set the challenge of green aviation, but the big corporations will not take the lead, as the risk to their existing business is too great. They need to be forced, through decisions made by society.

Twenty-first-century aviation pioneers will have a lot more advanced technology available to them than the early pioneers of flight, but they face two formidable problems. One, climate change, is not perceived to be a serious problem, so there is general apathy about the need for fundamental change in aviation. Two, there is a stifling regulatory framework that has to be overcome or dismantled.

In this chapter, mobilizing innovation to launch a new aviation industry is examined, based on the assumption that society looks on the industry from a neutral perspective and insists on changes to policy which will allow a new generation of entrepreneurs to transform the industry.

Launching a new aviation industry

The complex web of current regulations is out of date and has become an anchoring system that prevents green aviation taking off. What is needed is the freedom to expose the blue touchpaper and allow the circumstance where the spark of innovation from the pioneers is allowed to launch a new, sustainable aviation industry.

Modern pioneers are capable of leading a renaissance in aviation and capitalism can facilitate this, because there are hungry entrepreneurs snapping at the heels of the big corporations. When an industry stagnates into competing for slim margins in a mature market, an opportunity arises for new business models to take over. Aviation is an example of such an industry, trapped in an outdated policy framework, dominated by big airlines and big aircraft manufacturers. The capitalist way forward is not some grand plan to change the industry but the simple process of unleashing the entrepreneurs.

Mobilizing innovation

The next stage in aviation is a huge leap forward into the unknown. Examining carefully what has gone before, in order to plan where to go next, involves inherent inertia; this needs to be overcome by allowing the entrepreneurs to deliver proof of concept. The knowledge that something can be done brings a huge boost to those who follow. The first ascent of Mount Everest in 1953 by Edmund Hillary and Sherpa mountaineer Tenzing Norgay broke through the barrier of what was thought to be possible in mountaineering. Now anyone of moderate fitness and with modest climbing experience and £25,000 to spend can be escorted up the mountain. It is not risk free, but the route to follow has been established and a number of fixed ropes are left on the mountain. The peak has moved from an almost impossible challenge to being almost routine.

Proponents of green aviation, to succeed, will have to overcome barriers every bit as steep as the route up Mount Everest. I expect that in my lifetime flying in low-emission aircraft will become routine, but the aircraft and the infrastructure do not yet exist. If the world wants green aviation enough, and there is a push to overcome the barriers, it can be delivered.

The next generation of aviation pioneers need to work on the technology and the business models as well as understand how government policy and passenger attitudes will change. Flying will eventually become sustainable, comprising a complex collaboration between pilots, meteorologists and ground operation teams operating a new genus of air vehicle.

The action required to mobilize innovation will lead to dramatic changes in the industry and the pattern of how and when people fly. Once the proof-of-concept of green aviation has been delivered by flying prototypes, it will be followed by cheaper and better models as industry learns and economies of scale kick in. The prototypes will spark further innovation and start to shift customers' expectations. Green flying will cost significantly more at the outset, which will be a barrier, of course, but one that can be overcome. It all hinges on the priorities that policy-makers set and which passengers come to accept.

Stepping back to a neutral perspective

It is not in the interests of any of the current industry players to allow innovation free rein if this sends the message that the current fleet could become obsolete within a decade. If this idea took hold, the accountants, who have a responsibility to give a fair and accurate picture, could take billions off the balance sheets of airlines at the stroke of a pen.

The conventional view of the near-term future for aviation is that new sales will continue to be dominated by Boeing and Airbus, with the Dreamliner dominating the lower-capacity routes and the Airbus A380 taking the high-capacity long-haul routes like London to the Far East.

Over the next decade both companies hope to recoup their investment, but this is not assured. If action is taken to deal with the environmental impact of aviation, constraining capacity, the need will be for a very efficient mid-sized plane for long-haul flights. In these circumstances, a new plane based on Boeing's blended-wing technology might be the perfect option. If such a plane were built, it would dominate new sales but would also be a direct competitor for Boeing's current flagship model, the Dreamliner.

The commercial directors at both Boeing and Airbus will hope to dampen expectations of such a dramatically more efficient plane for a number of years yet. They have businesses to run and investment to recoup. However, society need not be sensitive to their commercial fortunes and should insist on sustainable aviation over a much shorter period.

Entrepreneurs waiting in the wings

In Chapter 11, a number of small entrepreneurial companies were mentioned that may be part of developing the future of green aviation and will be looking for capital. These are just a few of a large number of people and businesses with concepts for aviation. Most will not survive, for a variety of reasons: the idea doesn't work, the development is too slow or governments fail to establish a regulatory environment that supports and encourages low-emissions aviation. A small proportion of the entrepreneurs and inventors will succeed in launching their idea, either to grow into the corporations of the future or to be acquired by the established corporations as they reconfigure their capability portfolio to be able to compete in the new sustainable aviation industry.

The lifeblood of innovation is not just ideas but also investment capital, but investors need results. Venture capitalists will not apply their expertise and invest cash because of concerns over climate change; it is when the commercial opportunity looks capable of delivering a handsome profit that they will move into green aviation. However, a compelling business case cannot be developed for green aviation within the current regulatory and policy environment. The policy of open skies and tax-free fuel makes conventional aviation cheap, which sets an impossibly high hurdle for advanced green air vehicles to overcome to be competitive on price.

The most interesting ideas may not have surfaced yet, because the return on investment in green aviation, in the current policy framework, is not attractive. There is little incentive for the brightest brains in engineering and business to tackle the challenge or for venture capitalists to commit funds.

Innovation beyond aviation

Most analysis assumes that all the people and freight that now travel by conventional planes will, in the future, travel on green aircraft. This is the perspective that comes from inside the industry, with a view to growth and expansion. From the perspective of society, it becomes clear that this is a wrong assumption. The solution must include diverting people and freight to greener alternatives, with the greenest solution not to travel at all. Innovation in virtual reality conference facilities and short supply chain management are examples. There are many more areas of commerce which will thrive when the world grasps the nettle of forcing aviation to be green. Most of these are outside the scope of this book, but it is worth noting that there will be a whole range of unexpected developments that arise as conventional aviation is made obsolete. Focusing on aviation highlights the reasons not to act. Step back to a more neutral perspective and the future looks bright for a whole new batch of entrepreneurs and innovators.

One area where innovation has been stifled by cheap conventional aviation is transport by rail. The argument for green aviation is closely allied with the argument for a renaissance in railways.

14 | Short haul to trains

The twenty-first-century transport system will be a different mix of options to today's. There will be green air vehicles, airships and, for travel within countries and within continents, modern rail. Low-cost airlines have worked hard to persuade rail travellers off trains and into planes, an informal policy that is blind to the environmental consequences. The time has come to reverse this migration and persuade airline passengers back into railway carriages as one part of sustainable aviation policy (Bishop 2002). Roger Kemp of the Engineering Department of Lancaster University calculates that 'for high-density routes between major conurbations, such as Berlin to Brussels, London to Manchester or Köln to Amsterdam, air travel is always more environmentally damaging than rail travel. Whether CO_2 emissions are twice as high or 20 times as high, largely depends on the power source for the train' (Kemp 2009).

The future of short-haul flying is wrapped up with the future of green trains, therefore this short chapter is required to illustrate the changes in short-haul aviation not as a contraction in capacity (as seen from a narrow aviation focus), but as an improvement in the overall transport infrastructure.

The Cinderella of transport options

Long-distance trains have been the Cinderella of the transport system because they are slower than aircraft, require high levels of investment and have been seen as old fashioned compared with the glitz of flying. This is starting to change as high-quality trains build a positive image in passengers' minds, such as Japan's bullet trains, France's TGV,[1] the Eurostar service, which connects

---

1 France has an extensive fast train network: *Trains à Grande Vitesse* (TGV).

the UK with Europe through the Channel Tunnel, and Acela Express, Amtrak's high-speed rail service between Washington, DC, and Boston via New York.

Putting in place a train network that is a viable alternative to short-haul flying will take time. In the United States, President Obama has announced that 'Within 25 years, our goal is to give 80 percent of Americans access to high-speed rail' (Obama 2011). This is an ambitious target likely to require in excess of $500 billion. If much of this investment is to come from the private sector, the relative attractiveness of rail over short-haul flying will have to be addressed. In Britain, a collaboration between not-for-profit organizations and universities has proposed an ambitious target to eliminate domestic aviation by 2030 and replace it with trains (CAT 2010). However, the British government is finding that building new high-speed rail is proving slow and difficult. Chris Huhne, Secretary of State, Department for Energy and Climate Change, expressed his frustration in a comment that he expected China to be able to build 16,000 kilometres of high-speed rail in the time it takes Britain to build a high-speed line from London to Birmingham, a distance of 163 kilometres (Huhne 2011). This frustration may spread across the developed world with regret that investment in rail had not been initiated at the time of the 1970s oil crisis, in which event the infrastructure could be in place now. The opportunity should not be missed a second time.

In the developing world, where infrastructure is less mature, there is an opportunity to invest in rail but the economics are heavily skewed in favour of expanding short-haul aviation. In both the developed and the developing world, policy-makers need to understand the important role that trains have in a future sustainable transport system.

Investing in trains

The early days of the railways were marked by companies that raised money, laid rail tracks and later folded. The infrastructure remains in use hundreds of years later. For society it was a good investment, but it will be hard to persuade today's investors to follow the same path. Recent experience is not help-ful. The Channel Tunnel which connects Britain and France was built with government support but was designed as a private venture. The tunnel was completed in 1994 but only after costs ballooned from £4.7 billion to £9.5 billion. Under a mountain of debt, Eurotunnel came close to bankruptcy and was rescued in 2007 only by a massive debt restructuring operation that wrote off £3.4 billion of debts.

Railway infrastructure is very expensive to build but the infra-structure that results is valuable to society over the long term. The ground infrastructure for aviation requires less capital and is faster to build. When the focus is the cash needed upfront then aviation looks more attractive. This is particularly true for devel-oping countries wanting to build a new transport infrastructure quickly at least cost. Short-termism leads to short-haul flights; long-term planning should lead to green railways.

Railways have many more energy options than aviation, making them suitable for efficient low-carbon operations. One example, which is already being implemented across Europe and intro-duced into the United States (Amtrak 2010), is electric or hybrid locomotives. These can capture the energy from slowing down to feed back into the supply grid or to store in on-board batteries. Whether electric railways can be zero carbon depends on the source of the electricity. One possibility would be to fit solar PV collectors along the whole railway real estate, which can be considerable. For example, one kilometre of track might occupy real estate of 20 metres wide; that is 20,000 square metres of solar capacity; capture 150 watts of electricity per square metre, and the total energy generated could be 3,000 Kw. That is enough to power a typical electric locomotive. There could also be wind turbines, as the railway is already an intrusion into the natural environment so objections to collocation of wind turbines might be less vigorous. Embarking on a bold project to deliver a zero-carbon railway could become carbon negative because, on the rough calculation above, far more energy would be generated than would be required to run the trains.

Electrifying a track is expensive, but combining electrification and renewable energy supply in one project would have a number of synergies to spread the cost. Large renewable energy projects typically require investment in the power grid to connect supply with demand. Railway lines provide a ready route for the cabling required, and the trains draw power from close to the point of generation. This is an example of the sort of joined-up thinking that has to take place. The gantries for overhead cables and the framework for the solar panels can be one construction project.

Rail in the developing world

Rail should also have an important place in the developing world, but aviation is often the first choice in delivering long-distance transport infrastructure. Rail networks, which may date from colonial days, are in poor repair and the capital for repairs or new rail lines hard to find. It is easier to build airfields and encourage private companies to provide the fleets of aircraft. The low-cost aviation model is firmly established in the United States and Europe, providing an example for developing countries like India and China to follow. This is unfortunate because railway construction may well be suited to the populous developing world.

Rail networks take time to build and the construction is labour intensive, using technology that is suitable for local self-help. The new generation of efficient locomotives will use advanced technology, but breakdowns can be tolerated as local expertise is developed. This is not the case for aviation, where a breakdown is safety critical, so flight networks remain dependent on outside expertise for much longer.

Rail solutions require long-term planning, which has two key implications. First, rail is not a quick easy win; benefits take many years to feed through. Secondly, the decision to support rail has to be made early; key advisers like the World Bank should take note. Rail is proposed as the preferred long-term transport strategy for internal travel in the developing countries. It is less dependent on foreign technology and expertise, more in tune with the needs of a sustainable economy and, rather than committing to air networks built with foreign debt, the country can reap the benefits of long-term investment using a large local workforce.

There is an interesting job for aid organizations – to lead research into simple low-carbon rail technology. A concept that could be tested is a long train roofed with solar panels drawn by a hybrid locomotive. Railway lines tend not to have steep gradients and rapid acceleration is not generally a requirement for long-distance routes. An obvious limitation is that such a railway would operate only in daylight hours, but the technical barriers are few. The bigger barrier is the attitude that restricts investment in green rail and favours investment in aviation. Perhaps a philanthropic industrialist would like to take this idea through to proof-of-concept. At the very least it would be a public relations opportunity. If it works, it may become the future of transportation for sun-drenched countries.

Developing countries are not going to take kindly to the idea that they should hold back from massive expansion of their internal flight networks when they are simply aspiring to catch up with the US or European model. The developed world should show leadership by setting a clear policy that rail is the preferred option for journeys within a continent. This will then provide a different lead to the developing world so it can bounce past the stage of investment in airfields to start the long slow process of improving the rail network.

In Chapter 3, Liu Shaocheng, director of policy research at the Civil Aviation Administration of China, was reported predicting that airline passenger numbers in China would more than double to 700 million by 2020; and may double again to reach 1.5 billion by 2030. Liu Shaocheng, in the same speech, commented that the construction of high-speed railways in China and concerns about pollution may curb these long-term growth forecasts (Bloomberg 2010). This is a sign that China may take the decision to lead in showing how rail integrates into a sustainable transport system. China could overtake the United States and Europe, not just in terms of better domestic rail infrastructure, but also in terms of leadership in the technology required, if the developed world continues to shun investment in the railways.

Focus on long-term solutions

This short chapter on rail shows that policy to limit the environmental impact of short-haul flights should include support for the alternative of high-capacity, well-run green railways. The lead must come from government with policy that makes rail attractive to investors, including incentives as well as penalizing short-haul flying to make it relatively less attractive.

In the developing world, it may be tempting to follow the example of the rich countries, in allowing air networks to grow in order to achieve rapid improvement in the transport infrastructure; but this should be left to the private sector. The government's role, with responsibility for the overall transport system, should be to impose heavy taxation on aviation to channel investment into improving the rail network. Western aircraft manufacturers, eyeing potentially lucrative markets, will not like this policy suggestion, but developing countries should pursue national self-interest and aim for long-term solutions based on rail for internal transport connections.

15 | Global aviation policy framework

> What has yet to change is the willingness to take genuinely
> effective and substantive action in a coordinated way, at global
> level, such that no government perceives its national economic
> interests to be threatened. The mindset for this does not yet
> exist, but it must come.

This is the conclusion reached by Stefan Gössling and Paul Upham
in their examination of *Climate Change and Aviation* (2009). The
lack of willingness to take effective and substantive action is a
severe limitation on progress towards sustainable flying. It is
normal behaviour in the modern world to fly and not be concerned
about the consequences. You have to be a very sensitive person
to sit on a flight and feel guilty about the fumes coming out of
the engines. Each passenger is but one person among hundreds
on the flight. Each flight is but one among thousands each day
across the planet. Short-term individualism is a barrier to taking
effective collective action.

In this chapter, a policy framework is considered that brings
the long-term perspective to the core of aviation policy. The key
elements are taxation of aviation fuel – according to a new international agreement – and a policy for biofuel in aviation.

Long-term thinking

Long-term security and survival used to be at the heart of
managing human affairs. The great oak forests of Britain were
planted to ensure that the country would be able to build naval
ships in times of crisis. The people who planted the forests were
thinking ahead a century or more. Farmers would consider the
needs of their grandchildren or great-grandchildren when thinking about passing their land on to the next generation. Climate

change is a long-term threat to society and requires such forward deep thinking.

Now short-term thinking has taken over, often justified using the words of economist John Keynes: 'In the long run we are all dead' (Keynes 1923). I find this particularly interesting because it misrepresents Keynes. He actually wrote in the next sentence, 'Economists set themselves too easy, too useless a task if in tempestuous seasons they can only tell us that when the storm is past the ocean is flat again.' I shall rephrase his words for the modern world and its policy over climate change: In 2050 all the current senior policy-makers will be retired. Setting targets for carbon emissions out to 2050 is too easy, too useless a task.

The policy framework for aviation has to be framed around action in the near term that reaps benefits in the long term. Progress is stalled until world governments take the lead in changing policy.

Aviation within a sustainable policy framework

The future policy framework for aviation must fit within an overarching framework of sustainability. Current policy at world level is dominated by commitment to the free market but, as discussed in Chapter 7, this is incompatible with sustainability, so there is a need for a new foundation to policy.

The term I use for the new paradigm for the world economy is 'proximization'.[1] This involves bringing sustainability to the fore, putting the emphasis on local and regional solutions, reinforcing the state as the prime building block of world society, and ensuring that market economics are constrained to fit local circumstances. Proximization is a policy framework that fosters pride in identity and engagement with the locality and the local resource base, but is not a policy of isolationism. There will still be economic activity to balance resources between countries and regions but there will not be the massive unsustainable flows of

---

1 'Proximization' is a selfish determination to build sustainable societies, aimed at social provision and driven by economic policy, while minimizing adverse impacts on the environment (McManners 2008, 2010).

commodities and goods that have characterized globalization in recent decades.

Current aviation policy and globalization developed in parallel. The new policy for aviation should follow a similar dynamic and work in parallel with developing sustainable policy for the world. Aviation is highly regulated, and therefore easily controlled, so there is a strong argument to push for change that leads the policy agenda.

The precautionary principle

The precautionary principle is useful in guiding policy and is well established in aviation. A new design is put through intensive computer simulation. If this exposes a risk of failure, engineers change the design. When the theoretical design is shown to be safe it moves to production and flight testing. The first flights are undertaken by test pilots, providing a further chance to address flaws in the design before rolling it out for widespread use.

The precautionary principle also has its place in climate policy. Computer simulation models are used to predict the likely outcomes of a range of CO_2 emissions scenarios. These warn that human society is causing changes to the climate and it is possible that the changes could be disastrous. But, as with the first flight of a new aircraft, there is no way to be sure whether the climate will perform in accordance with the computer models. When CO_2 in the atmosphere passes the levels used in the models we will know the consequences first-hand.

For the atmosphere, there is no possibility of a prototype to carry out a final check on the results coming out of the computer simulation. The experiment being undertaken with the atmosphere applies to the Earth, the ecosystem and all the peoples of the world. A high-carbon atmosphere cannot be sent back to the factory for a redesign. As the world continues to emit high levels of CO_2 it is not just the life of a test pilot being put at risk; it is not just a prototype that might crash. Ignoring the warnings of the computer climate simulations puts whole regions at risk of localized ecosystem collapse, particularly in vulnerable parts of the world like sub-Saharan Africa and low-lying countries like Bangladesh; but no population should be confident that they will not be affected. Climate refugees and disruption to agriculture will be problems the world will share.

Climate change may be serious or it may not, but whatever will happen cannot be backtracked on. It is like a plane taking off – once it has gone a certain distance down the runway and reached take-off speed it has to become airborne and cannot land until it has had time to complete a circuit of the airfield to get back to the runway. A circuit of the airfield for the climate could be a century or more to return CO_2 levels back to pre-industrial levels. It is folly to continue to accelerate down the runway of fossil-fuel dependency despite scientists predicting the likelihood of a crash. No aircraft manufacturer or airline would take such a risk.

The forum for change

The Chicago Convention was an ad hoc meeting called specifically to 'discuss the principles and methods to be followed in the adoption of a new aviation convention' (ICAO 2010b). Over sixty-five years later, another such meeting is long overdue, but it will come about only if world leaders call for it.

The G8[2] group of countries is one forum where action could be initiated to set in train the negotiation of a new convention. The forum was instigated by the United States following the 1973 oil crisis; it would return the G8 close to its roots to discuss action in response to the current climate crisis. The problem for the G8, as an exclusive club, is that it lacks perceived legitimacy, with a history of attracting violent protest from the anti-globalization movement. G8 leaders represent some of the world's most powerful economies; if this group found a way to introduce a mechanism to constrain the emissions from aviation, this could bolster the reputation of its members among a broad lobby of all those concerned about climate change at home and abroad.

2 Formed as the G6: France, Germany, Italy, Japan, the United Kingdom and the United States; it became the G7 with the inclusion of Canada and the G8 when Russia joined in 1997.

The larger G20[3] group of countries is more likely to be the forum that initiates action rather than either the UN or the G8. Talks brokered by the UN have the most legitimacy but also the most inertia. Discussions in the G8 can move quickly but fail to engage wide support. The G20 is representative of the world community with members from all the continents of the world, yet small enough to broker a deal without delay. A series of climate-related events that underline climate change as a crisis, in the period leading up to a G20 meeting, could indeed be the trigger to call for a new convention on civil aviation.

The G20 was established in 1999 as a response to both the financial crisis of the late 1990s and a growing recognition that key emerging-market countries were not adequately included in the core of global economic discussion and governance. A decade after it was formed it is earning a reputation for influencing policy. At the G20 meeting in London in April 2009, in the wake of the worst financial crisis since the 1930s, a range of measures were agreed. The final statement agreed at the meeting began: 'We face the greatest challenge to the world economy in modern times; a crisis which has deepened since we last met, which affects the lives of women, men, and children in every country, and which all countries must join together to resolve. A global crisis requires a global solution.'

Insert the word 'climate' before the word 'crisis' and this could be the opening sentence of a statement on the pending climate crisis. The closing words of the 2009 statement were: 'We have committed ourselves to work together with urgency and determination to translate these words into action. We agreed to meet again before the end of this year to review progress on our commitments.'

The twenty-six paragraphs between the opening and closing paragraphs contained a wide range of measures to bolster the world financial system. These provided clear direction to

3 G20: G8 + Argentina, Australia, Brazil, China, India, Indonesia, Mexico, Saudi Arabia, South Africa, Republic of Korea, Turkey and the European Union.

governments and global institutions such as the IMF. Such statements are not legally binding in themselves, which is why leaders can agree such a plan in a few short days. This has parallels in business when chief executives agree the 'heads of terms' of a deal. This lays down what has been agreed in principle and sets the context within which the lawyers and other executives work out the detail. Issues can still arise that prevent the deal going through but the 'heads of terms' is the important first stage involving the key leaders at the top of the corporations meeting face to face.

The world needs the G20 to bring the climate crisis on to its agenda and agree a 'heads of terms' over what is to be done. One of the items for action is to convene a new convention on civil aviation, the outline parameters for which are discussed below.

Policy for the transition

While negotiating a new convention, the existing policy framework will have to remain in place under the administration of the ICAO. Although the current policy framework is out of date, it contains a wealth of regulations that have evolved over the years. As the core structure of a new convention emerges, based on a new set of principles, it is likely that there will be huge chunks of existing policy that will fit inside the new framework. Although I suggest that it will not be feasible to change the current convention from within, starting anew does not mean abandoning all that has gone before.

New policy foundations

I propose the following headline objective of the Convention on Sustainable Civil Aviation: 'The aim of a new convention would be to foster the future development of sustainable international civil aviation to help to create and promote cooperation that contributes to the sustainability of world society.'

Beneath this prime objective I suggest outline policy for the two key areas of the policy framework: aviation fuel tax and the introduction of biofuel.

Policy for aviation fuel tax Tax-free aviation fuel is an anachronism that should be removed from the new policy framework. This requires international coordination so countries can move in concert to avoid jeopardizing the commercial prospects of businesses within their jurisdiction.

The underlying principle of the aviation fuel tax is to set a firm floor for investment decisions over next decade and beyond. It is proposed that a minimum rate should be agreed for the tax on aviation fuel for international flights, with countries having the freedom to impose a higher rate. For political reasons, the tax should start low to embed the principle in international aviation policy, but then rise according to an escalator published years ahead and enshrined in the new convention.

A key responsibility of the organization overseeing the new convention will be the fiendishly difficult task of brokering agreement over setting the floor tax rate. Very low rates have been considered by researchers examining fuel tax from a revenue perspective, who note that a high rate encourages airlines to change the way they operate, thus using less fuel so less overall tax is collected (Keen and Strand 2006, 2007). This is not a worry because the proposal is not primarily a tax-raising measure but rather a tax lever to drive a transformation in the industry; burning less fuel is part of the desirable outcome and a natural consequence of setting a tax rate sufficiently high to drive change.

A pitfall to avoid is the temptation to collect the tax centrally to fund development, as suggested by Jha (2002), Atkinson (2005) and the new economics foundation (nef 2008). Governments are more likely to support an aviation fuel tax if they retain the tax receipts and make their own decisions over how to apply the income.

Biofuel policy Research into biofuels for aviation should continue, both to foster understanding of the wider implications for the world energy infrastructure and to meet the exacting safety standards for fuels used in aviation, such as the requirement not to freeze at the low temperatures found at high altitude. Despite the need for further research, enough is known to set policy for the medium term, providing the aviation industry, and its wide network of suppliers, with clear guidance for future developments.

The most advanced biofuels, often referred to as third- or fourth-generation biofuels, will have a useful future role in aviation and policy should support further development. Such fuels can be produced in desert regions so there is no clash with food, and it is hard to envisage the production facilities expanding to such an extent that the supply of the world's deserts is exhausted. There are technical and sustainability challenges to overcome, but the main barrier is economic; advanced biofuels will be expensive and will not be produced in large quantities without change to the economic parameters.

The policy for biofuels to support the development of sustainable aviation should be set within the wider context of the challenge facing society of breaking dependence on fossil fuel. Current knowledge would suggest that support for the development of advanced biofuels would be appropriate. As taxes are increased on aviation fuel, advanced biofuels should be taxed less, or not at all during the early years to kick-start development. This exemption would need to be kept under review with respect to how energy use patterns evolve and the degree of success in decarbonization across the whole of society. It seems certain that demand for biofuel will outstrip demand across the economy, in which case tax exemption for biofuel in aviation should be withdrawn once the technology for advanced biofuels is mature.

Clear and unambiguous policy for biofuel, that recognizes the limitations, will prevent the aviation business from wasting resources undertaking nugatory development work. The policy should provide support in the near term for the development of third-generation biofuel for which there is neither conflict with food production nor a requirement to take land that is needed for the preservation of biodiversity. Such development should remain subject to review as research expands knowledge of their place within the energy systems of society. Policy should state explicitly that there will be no exemption from aviation fuel tax for first- and second-generation biofuels.

Space – the final frontier The new convention on aviation may stay in place as long as the Chicago Convention, taking the industry towards the close of this century. It should therefore include policy for civil flights beyond the atmosphere and into space. It would be logical to support, in principle, the development of the civil space sector, as the sustainable long-term future for human society will include establishing colonies on other planets. This would have parallels with the way the Chicago Convention was designed to underpin expansion and growth of the new technology of that era. The replacement convention must put the past behind, ensure that mass aviation is brought under effective control and introduce new incentives for the next big surge of innovation.

Civil space technology should not be given carte blanche to ignore its environmental impact. For example, it would be iniquitous to exclude space vehicles from fuel taxation because the early space passengers will be the mega-rich. However, the principle of encouragement for civil transport to expand into space should be enshrined in the new convention, with the detail evolving over the coming decades.

Forcing the transition

Globalization and aviation are both heading towards a transition. I expect that globalization will be replaced by the paradigm of proximization, in which sustainability is put at the core of policy-making. Applying the policies of sustainability will inevitably force aviation to pay the full cost of its environmental impact. One choice available to policy-makers is to delay change in aviation until a later stage, when sustainability is better understood. This would avoid a tough fight with powerful vested interests but would also be an abrogation of responsibility. Getting agreement for international sustainable aviation policy will require breaking the mould of current policy. It will be difficult and disruptive, but also necessary; the sooner a start is made the less traumatic the transition will be.

Conclusion

> Air travel has brought many benefits to modern life. Let us
> ensure that, from now on, it benefits both people and the
> planet. Ban Ki-moon (ICAO 2010d)

Aviation is trapped in an outdated policy framework which ensures
that aviation is largely exempt from policy to control carbon
dioxide emissions.

It is the nature of society to wait until forced to act. It is
therefore likely that the environmental impact of aviation will have
to become a real crisis before action is taken. This is unfortunate
because the action necessary is not hard to identify, and the
outcome is better for society. Despite the evident benefits, there
are powerful vested interests in opposition, concerned about the
near-term economic impacts. In a world that puts the emphasis
on short-term outcomes, this is hard to resolve, but such concerns
should not be allowed to block progress.

The aviation industry is built on the false premise of cheap
fuel. It is not possible to address adequately emissions from aviation without challenging this assumption. Society will have to be
weaned off fossil fuel; either because supplies run low or because
the environmental impact is too great. The ecosystem is under
pressure, leading to climate change, which will have damaging
consequences if the world does not reduce CO_2 emissions. It is
not known exactly how great the damage will be. In the words of
The Economist (2010a): 'Action on climate is justified, not because
the science is certain, but precisely because it is not.' The possibility that climate change may be less severe than scientists
predict has to be balanced against the possibility that it could
be worse, with tragic consequences.

Attempts to control CO_2 emissions have not been effective, with too much expectation of a global agreement to limit overall emissions. While negotiations continue, there is the impression that a solution is pending, providing an excuse for countries to await the outcome. The focus of the UN-brokered climate talks is on targets, which are proving very difficult to agree, but this is the easy stage because delivering the targets will be even harder.

To break the world's addiction to oil will require a step-change in the way that society operates. The necessary changes are complex and interconnected, affecting all aspects of people's lives and lifestyles. As sustainability becomes the foundation of policy, the built environment, manufacturing and agriculture will have to change together with altered dynamics of trade and investment.

Transportation, in particular, will go through a transformation as transport on the roads, on the ocean and in the air has to migrate away from using fossil fuel. The sustainable solution is less fossil-fuel-powered transport and more green transportation, with most progress being achieved through redesigning society and the economy to reduce the need for so much transportation.

Continuation of business-as-usual will take the planet to dangerously high levels of atmospheric CO_2. The developed world is at the beginning of the process of reducing emissions. If the transition is slow, the rest of the world will follow the same well-trodden path. There will continue to be a huge expansion of global CO_2 emissions, even as the developed world slowly squeezes carbon out of their economies. The poorer countries do not want to forgo their modernization, following the example of industrialization based on fossil fuel. There is no reason for the developing world to hold back, when the main perpetrators of CO_2 emissions over many decades are doing so little to lead change.

The developed world has to provide bold leadership to demonstrate that a low-carbon society is both feasible and better. A clear commitment to decarbonizing society, to testing and proving alternative solutions, opens the possibility that less developed countries will step off the conventional development track and leapfrog ahead to the sustainable future to which we all must aspire.

Conclusion

165

Aviation serves the rich world and the affluent people of the poor world. It is not vital to society and the economy, despite claims from many quarters. Forcing aviation into a sustainable policy framework would be to force change on the rich world, sending a loud and clear message: the developed world can, and will, tackle CO_2 emissions.

The action required is a mechanism that can both reduce the demand for conventional aviation and support the migration of the industry away from fossil fuel. To achieve both these ends requires taxation of aviation fuel, not proxy taxes such as departure taxes or passenger taxes, but a tax that falls directly on fossil fuel. It is time that politicians stopped tiptoeing around this central issue. This will require agreement among a group of countries that are willing to defend their collective economic interests through levying additional charges on flights from any country that chooses to remain outside the agreement. The purpose of the tax should not be muddled, to ensure that the aims are achieved: to impose contraction on conventional aviation and enable a strong business case for the development of green air vehicles. The tax can start low, as the principle is introduced, but should rise quickly to fulfil the aims.

The tax receipts would be considerable and could be used for sustainable infrastructure, such as low-carbon ground transportation, or any number of other purposes, including aid to regions badly affected by climate change. Discussion over collecting such tax at the global level should be avoided as it risks stalling the whole process. The agreement to levy an aviation fuel tax has to have global reach, but collecting the tax and deciding how it is spent should be left to national arrangements. There are four tasks that world leaders need to be persuaded to consider:

- first, accept that aviation is not a special case for exemption from environmental regulations;
- secondly, put aviation on the agenda of the G20, a group that represents all the continents of the world yet is small enough to take decisions;

- thirdly, decide that an early transition to sustainable aviation would demonstrate that the world is serious about tackling CO_2 emissions;
- fourthly, agree in principle among the members of the G20 that a tax on aviation fuel is desirable and instigate a new convention on civil aviation to work out how it could be implemented.

The looming dangers of climate change mean that policy for aviation has to shift from support for continued expansion to focus on reducing the sector's environmental impact. This should not be resisted; it will be a positive move forward, resulting in the launch of the third golden age of aviation.

References

ACI (2009) 'ACI World Airport Traffic Report (WATR) 2009', Montreal: Airports Council International.

Aeros (2010) 'Our company', www.aerosml.com.

Airbus (2010) 'Biomimicry', www.airbus.com/innovation/eco-efficiency/design/biomimicry.

Amtrak (2010) 'Amtrak awards $466 million contract for 70 new electric locomotives', Amtrak press release, 29 October.

Anderson, J., I. Skinner, C. Bausch and A. Leipprand (2006) 'Reducing the impact of aviation on climate change: economic aspects of inclusion of the aviation sector in the EU Emissions Trading Scheme', Briefing Note IP/A/ENVI/NT/2006-08, Brussels: European Parliament.

Atkinson, A. B. (2005) New Sources of Development Finance, Oxford: Oxford University Press.

Aviationexplorer (2010) 'Boeing 797 aircraft', www.aviationexplorer.com/boeing_797_aircraft_facts.html.

BBC (2008a) 'Zoom Airlines suspend all flights', BBC News, online, 28 August, news.bbc.co.uk/1/hi/scotland/glasgow_and_west/7586654.stm.

— (2008b) 'Airline in first bio-fuel flight', BBC News, online, 24 February, news.bbc.co.uk/1/hi/7261214.stm.

Bishop, S. (2002) 'Sustainable aviation policy', New Economy, 9(3): 143–7.

Bisignani, G. (2007) 'Speech to the Annual General Meeting of the Arab Air Carriers' Organisation', Damascus, Syria, 24 October 2007.

— (2010) 'State of the air transport industry', Speech at the 66th IATA Annual General Meeting and World Air Transport Summit, Berlin, 7 June.

Black, S. (2008) Eco-Chic: The Fashion Paradox, London: Black Dog.

Bloomberg (2010) 'China airline passengers may double to 700 million by 2020, regulator says', Bloomberg News, online, 8 July, www.bloomberg.com/news/2010-07-08/china-airline-passengers-may-double-to-700-million-by-2020-regulator-says.html.

Boeing (2007) 'Boeing celebrates the premiere of the 787 Dreamliner', Boeing press release, 8 July.

— (2010) 'History of Boeing and the Everett site', www.boeing.com/commercial/facilities/index.html.

Bows, A., K. Anderson and S. Mander (2009) 'Aviation in turbulent times', *Technology Analysis and Strategic Management*, 21(1): 17–37.

Brannigan, C., V. Paschos, C. Eyers and J. Wood (2009) 'Report on International Aviation and Maritime Emissions in a Copenhagen (post 2012) Agreement, Final Report', Report by AEA for Department for Transport (DfT), June, London: Department for Transport.

CAA (2008) 'Recent trends in growth of UK air passenger demand', Report, January, UK: Civil Aviation Authority.

Calder, S. (2006) *No Frills: The Truth behind the Low-Cost Revolution in the Skies*, London: Virgin.

Carson, R. (1962) *Silent Spring*, Boston, MA: Houghton Mifflin.

CAT (2010) 'Zero carbon Britain 2030: a new energy strategy', UK: Centre for Alternative Technology.

Cavanagh, J. and J. Mander (2004) *Alternatives to Economic Globalization: A Better World Is Possible*, 2nd edn, San Francisco, CA: Berrett-Koehler.

CBO (2005) 'Options for Strategic Military Transportation Systems', Congressional Budget Office Study, Washington, DC: Congress of the United States.

China Business Review (2011) 'Aviation', *China Business Review*, 38(1): 8.

Clarke, J. (2010) 'Creating en route (cruise) trajectories that have minimal impact on the environment', ICAO Colloquium on Aviation and Climate Change, 11–14 May, Montreal, www.icao.int/CLQ10/Docs/4_Clarke.pdf.

Czipura, C. and D. R. Jolly (2007) 'Global airline alliances: sparking profitability for a troubled industry', *Journal of Business Strategy*, 28(2): 57–64.

De Bono, A., P. Peduzzi, S. Kluser and G. Giuliani (2004) 'Impacts of summer 2003 heat wave in Europe', *UNEP Environment Alert Bulletin*, Nairobi: UNEP.

Djoghlaf, A. (2010) 'Statement by Mr Ahmed Djoghlaf, the Executive Secretary of the Convention on Biological Diversity on the Occasion of the 2nd International Conference on Sustainable Business and Consumption, 15 June 2010, Nuremberg, Germany', Montreal: UNEP (Convention on Biological Diversity).

Doganis, R. (2001) *The Airline Business in the 21st Century*, London: Routledge.

— (2010) *Flying Off Course: Airline Economics and Marketing*, 4th edn, London: Routledge.

Dunlap, R. E. and A. G. Mertig (eds) (1992) *American Environmentalism: The U.S. Environmental Movement, 1970–1990*, Washington, DC: Taylor & Francis.

Eclipse Aerospace (2010) 'The Eclipse 500', eclipseaerospace.

net/files/pdf/Eclipse500_
Brochure.pdf.

Economist (2010a) 'Spin, science and climate change', *The Economist*, 18 March.

— (2010b) 'Powering up', The Economist Technology Quarterly, *The Economist*, 4 September.

EIA (2011) 'International Energy Statistics', www.eia.gov.

EU (2008) 'Directive 2008/101/EC of the European Parliament and of the Council', *Official Journal of the European Union*, Brussels: EU, 19 November.

European Commission (1987) 'Council Regulation (EEC) No. 3975/87 of 14 December 1987, laying down the procedure for the application of the rules on competition to undertakings in the air transport sector', Brussels: European Commission.

Fairtrade (2010) 'What is Fair Trade?', www.fairtrade.org.uk/ what_is_fairtrade/faqs.aspx.

Fullerton, D., A. Leicester and S. Smith (2010) 'Environmental taxes', in J. Mirrlees et al. (eds), *Dimensions of Tax Design: The Mirrlees Review*, Oxford: Oxford University Press, pp. 485–8.

General Accounting Office (1997) 'B-2 Bomber: Cost and Operational Issues (Letter Report, 08/14/97, GAO/NSIAD-97-181)', United States: General Accounting Office.

Gore, A. (2006) *An Inconvenient Truth: The Planetary Emergency of Global Warming and What We Can Do about It*, New York: Bloomsbury.

Gössling, S. and P. Upham (2009) *Climate Change and Aviation: Issues, Challenges and Solutions*, London: Earthscan.

Heinberg, R. (2005) *The Party's Over: Oil, war and the fate of industrial societies*, 2nd edn, UK: Clairview Books.

Holloway, S. (2008) *Straight and Level: Practical Airline Economics*, UK: Ashgate.

House of Commons (2007) 'The Voluntary Carbon Offset Market', House of Commons Environmental Audit Committee, Sixth Report of Session 2006–07, HC 331, London: House of Commons, 23 July.

— (2008) 'Pre-Budget Report 2008: Green fiscal policy in a recession', House of Commons Environmental Audit Committee, Third Report of Session 2008–09, HC 202, London: House of Commons, 16 March.

Howard, F. (1998) *Wilbur and Orville: A Biography of the Wright Brothers*, US: Dover Publications.

Huhne, C. (2011) Keynote speech at 'A Perfect Storm Ahead? Geographical perspectives on food, water and energy security to 2030', Royal Geographical Society, London, 17 February.

Hybrid Air Vehicles (2010) 'Environmental impact', www.hybridairvehicles.net/ company_environmental. html.

IATA (2007) 'Passenger numbers to reach 2.75 billion by 2011', Press release, 24 October.

— (2010a) 'Next steps for Indian aviation – developing a common vision', Press release, 23 September.

— (2010b) 'The World Air Transport Statistics (WATS) 54th Edition', www.iata.org/ps/publications/Pages/wats.aspx, accessed 28 February 2011.

— (2010c) 'International Air Transport Association Annual Report 2010', Montreal: IATA.

— (2011) 'Fuel price analysis', www.iata.org/whatwedo/economics/fuel_monitor/Pages/price_analysis.aspx, accessed 28 February.

ICAO (2000) 'ICAO's policies on taxation in the field of international air transport', 3rd edn, ICAO Document 8632, Montreal: International Civil Aviation Organization.

— (2006) 'Convention on International Civil Aviation', 9th edn, ICAO Doc 7300/9, Montreal: International Civil Aviation Organization.

— (2008) 'Guidance on the use of emissions trading for aviation', 1st edn, ICAO Doc 9885, Montreal: International Civil Aviation Organization.

— (2010a) 'History: the beginning', www.icao.int/cgi/goto_m.pl?icao/en/hist/history01.htm.

— (2010b) 'International Civil Aviation Conference', Chicago, IL, 1 November–7 December 1944, www.icao.int/icao/en/chicago_conf/index.html.

— (2010c) 'Assembly – 37th Session, Report of the Executive Committee, on Agenda Item 17 (Section on Climate Change)', A37-WP/402, P/66, Montreal: International Civil Aviation Organization.

— (2010d) 'ICAO Environmental Report 2010', Montreal: International Civil Aviation Organization.

IEA (2010) CO_2 *Emissions from Fuel Combustion Highlights* (2010 edn), International Energy Agency.

Inderwildi, O., C. Carey, G. Santos and X. Yan (2010) *Future of Mobility Road Map*, 2nd edn, Oxford: SSEE.

IPCC (2007) 'Summary for policymakers', in S. Solomon, D. Qin, M. Manning, Z. Chen, M. Marquis, K. B. Averyt, M Tignor and H. L. Miller (eds), *Climate Change 2007: The Physical Science Basis. Contribution of Working Group I to the Fourth Assessment Report of the Intergovernmental Panel on Climate Change*, Cambridge: Cambridge University Press.

Jha, R. (2002) 'Innovative sources of development finance: global cooperation in the twenty-first century', WIDER Discussion Paper 2002/98, Helsinki: United Nations University, World Institute for Development Economic Research.

Kahn Ribeiro, S. and S. Kobayashi (coordinating lead authors)

(2007) 'Transport and its infrastructure', in *Climate Change 2007: Mitigation. Contribution of Working Group III to the Fourth Assessment Report of the Intergovernmental Panel on Climate Change*, Cambridge: Cambridge University Press.

Kar, R., P. A. Bonnefoy and R. J. Hansman (2010) 'Dynamics of implementation of mitigating measures to reduce CO_2 emissions from commercial aviation', Report no. ICAT-2010-01, Cambridge, MA: MIT International Center for Air Transportation, June.

Kay, W. (2010) 'Top guns fly on algae in the US battle for fuel', *Sunday Times*, 12 September.

Keen, M. J. and J. Strand (2006) 'Indirect taxes on international aviation', IMF Working Paper WP/06/124, Washington, DC: International Monetary Fund.

— (2007) 'Indirect taxes on international aviation', *Fiscal Studies*, 28: 1–41.

Kemp, R. (2009) 'Short-haul aviation – under what conditions is it more environmentally benign than the alternatives?', *Technology Analysis and Strategic Management*, 21(1): 115–27.

Keynes, J. M. (1923) *A Tract on Monetary Reform*, London: Macmillan.

King, D. A. (2004) 'Climate change science: adapt, mitigate, or ignore?', *Science*, 303(5655): 176–7.

Knabb, R. D., J. R. Rhome and D. P. Brown (2005) 'Hurricane Katrina 23–30 August 2005', Tropical Cyclone Report, Miami, FL: National Hurricane Center, 20 December, updated 10 August 2006.

Kriegler, E., J. W. Hall, H. Held, R. Dawson and H. J. Schellnhuber (2009) 'Imprecise probability assessment of tipping points in the climate system', *Proceedings of the National Academy of Sciences*, 106(13): 5041–6.

Layard, R. (2005) *Happiness: Lessons from a New Science*, London: Allen Lane.

Levine, J. (2008) *On a Wing and a Prayer*, London: Collins.

Lindbergh, C. A. (1948) *Of Flight and Life*, New York: Scribner's Sons.

— (1964) 'Is civilization progress?', *Reader's Digest*, July.

Lufthansa (2010) 'Shareholder structure', investor-relations. lufthansa.com/en/aktie/ shareholder-structure.html.

Lüthi, D., M. Le Floch, B. Bereiter et al. (2008) 'High-resolution carbon dioxide concentration record 650,000–800,000 years before present', *Nature*, 453: 379–82.

Lynas, M. (2007) *Six Degrees: Our Future on a Hotter Planet*, London: Fourth Estate.

Maniatis, K., M. Weitz and A. Zschocke (2011) '2 million tons per year: A performing biofuels supply chain for EU aviation', Technical paper June 2011 [available at: http://ec.europa.eu/energy/

technology/initiatives/doc/
20110622_biofuels_flight_path_
technical_paper.pdf].

McCraw, T. K. (1984) *Prophets of
Regulation: Charles Francis
Adams, Louis D. Brandeis, James
M. Landis, Alfred E. Kahn*, Cam-
bridge, MA: Harvard University
Press.

McManners, P. J. (2008) *Adapt and
Thrive: The Sustainable Revolution*, UK: Susta Press.

— (2009) *Victim of Success:
Civilization at Risk*, UK: Susta
Press.

— (2010) *Green Outcomes in the
Real World: Global Forces, Local
Circumstances and Sustainable
Solutions*, UK: Gower.

Meadows, D. H., D. L. Meadows
and J. Randers (1972) *The
Limits to Growth*, New York:
Universe Books.

Meadows, D. H., J. Randers and
D. Meadows (2004) *Limits to
Growth: The 30-Year Update*,
Vermont: Chelsea Green Pub-
lishing Company.

Meehl, G. A. and T. F. Stocker
(2007) 'Global climate
projections', in S. Solomon,
D. Qin, M. Manning, Z. Chen,
M. Marquis, K. B. Averyt,
M. Tignor and H. L. Miller
(eds), *Climate Change 2007:
The Physical Science Basis.
Contribution of Working Group I
to the Fourth Assessment Report
of the Intergovernmental Panel
on Climate Change*, Cambridge:
Cambridge University Press.

Meinshausen, M., N. Mein-
shausen, W. Hare, S. Raper,
K. Frieler, R. Knutti, D. J.
Frame and R. Allen (2009)
'Greenhouse-gas emission
targets for limiting global
warming to 2 degrees C',
Nature, 458, 30 April.

Merejkowski, D. (1901) *The
Romance of Leonardo da Vinci*,
vol. II, New York: G. P. Put-
nam's Sons.

Met Office (2009) '"Noughties"
confirmed as the warmest decade on record', Press release,
9 December.

— (2010) 'Cumbria floods November 2009 – a look back',
www.metoffice.gov.uk/about-
us/who/how/case-studies/
cumbria-floods.

Millennium Ecosystem Assess-
ment (2005) *Ecosystems and
Human Well-being: Synthesis*,
Washington, DC: Island Press.

Murray, J. (2010) 'UN climate chief
warns 2020 carbon targets will
be missed', www.business-
green.com/bg/news/1802850/
un-climate-chief-warns-2020
-carbon-targets-missed, 8 June.

NASA (2000) 'Small aircraft
propulsion: the future is here',
NASA Fact Sheet FS-2000-04-
001-GRC, March.

— (2009) 'X-48B blended wing-
body', Fact sheet, www.nasa.
gov/centers/dryden/news/
FactSheets/FS-090-DFRC.html,
April.

nef (2008) 'Plane truths: do the
economic arguments for
aviation growth really fly?',
London: new economics
foundation.

Norris, G. (2010) 'Testbed tempo', *Aviation Week*, 24 May, p. 4.

Nsouli, S. M. (2008) 'Ensuring a sustainable and inclusive globalization', Speech by the Director, Offices in Europe, International Monetary Fund, at the Universal Postal Union Congress, Geneva, 25 July.

Obama, B. (2011) State of the Union Address to Congress, Washington, DC, 25 January.

OECD (2010) *Globalisation, Transport and the Environment*, Paris: OECD Publishing.

Peeters, P. M., J. Middel and A. Hoolhorst (2005) 'Fuel efficiency of commercial aircraft: an overview of historical and future trends', Report NLR-CR-2005-669, Amsterdam: National Aerospace Laboratory NLR, November.

Pope, V., F. Carroll, D. Britton and J. Lowe (2008) 'Avoiding dangerous climate change', Report 08/0287, UK: Met Office (Hadley Centre).

Power-technology (2010) 'Whitelee Wind Farm, Scotland, United Kingdom', www.power-technology.com/projects/whiteleewindfarm.

Pratt & Whitney (2010) 'Burns less fuel', www.purepowerengine.com/fuel_burn.html.

Saleh, W. and G. Sammer (eds) (2009) *Travel Demand Management and Road User Pricing: Success, Failure and Feasibility*, UK: Ashgate.

Scottish Green Energy Awards (2009) 'Whitelee Wind Farm won the "Best Renewable Project Award" at the Scottish Green Energy Awards 2009', www.greenenergyawards.co.uk.

SDC (2008) 'Breaking the holding pattern: a new approach to aviation policymaking in the UK', London: Sustainable Development Commission, May.

Sims, R. and M. Taylor (2008) 'From 1st- to 2nd-generation biofuel technologies: an overview of current industry and RD&D activities', Paris: IEA.

Solomon, S., D. Qin, M. Manning, Z. Chen, M. Marquis, K. B. Averyt, M. Tignor and H. L. Miller (eds) (2007) *Contribution of Working Group I to the Fourth Assessment Report of the Intergovernmental Panel on Climate Change, 2007*, Cambridge: Cambridge University Press.

Stern, N. (2007) *The Economics of Climate Change: The Stern Review*, Cambridge: Cambridge University Press.

Sukhdev, P. and S. Stone (2010) 'Green economy: driving a green economy through public finance and fiscal policy reform', Working Paper Version 1.0, Geneva: UNEP (Division of Technology, Industry and Economics).

Tans, P. (2010) 'Trends in atmospheric carbon dioxide – Mauna Loa', www.esrl.noaa.gov/gmd/ccgg/trends, accessed 28 February 2011.

Thoreau, H. D. (1861) Journal

entry for 3 January 1861, www.library.ucsb.edu/thoreau/writings_journals33.html.

UKCCC (2009) 'Meeting the UK aviation target – options for reducing emissions to 2050', UK: Committee on Climate Change.

UNESCO (2009) *Climate Change and Arctic Sustainable Development: Scientific, social, cultural and educational challenges*, Paris: UNESCO.

UNFCCC (1998) 'Kyoto Protocol to the United Nations Framework Convention on Climate Change', Bonn: UNFCCC.

— (2010) 'Outcome of the work of the Ad Hoc Working Group on long-term Cooperative Action under the Convention', Draft decision CP 16, advance unedited version, unfccc.int, accessed 28 February 2011.

Vasigh, B., K. Fleming and T. Tacker (2008) *Introduction to Air Transport Economics: From Theory to Applications*, UK: Ashgate.

Wainwright, M. (2010) 'Cockermouth floods: one year on and business is booming', *Guardian*, 19 November.

Walker, S. and M. Cook (2009)

'The contested concept of sustainable aviation', *Sustainable Development*, 17(6): 378–90.

WCED (1987) *Our Common Future*, Oxford: Oxford University Press.

Willerslev, E., E. Cappellini, W. Boomsma et al. (2007) 'Ancient biomolecules from deep ice cores reveal a forested southern Greenland', *Science*, 317(5834): 111–14.

Woodin, M. and C. Lucas (2004) *Green Alternatives to Globalization: A Manifesto*, London: Pluto Press.

WTTC (2009a) 'The travel industry sets the standards on climate change', Joint communiqué from the WTTC and UNWTO, press release, 11 December.

— (2009b) 'Leading the challenge on climate change', WTTC Report, London: World Travel & Tourism Council, 1 February.

X PRIZE Foundation (2010) 'Ansari X PRIZE', space.xprize.org/ansari-x-prize.

Yeager, C., B. Cardenas, B. Hoover, J. Russell and J. Young (1997) *The Quest for Mach One: A First-Person Account of Breaking the Sound Barrier*, New York: Penguin Studio.

Index

Index